The Futile System

How to unchain Congress
and make the system work again

John J. Rhodes

Congressional reform is like the weather. Everybody talks about it but nobody does anything about it—nobody except a man with the kind of fortitude that has made John J. Rhodes the leader of his party in the U.S. House of Representatives.

Time and again Rhodes has marshaled his minority forces, lopsidedly outnumbered by the Democratic majority, to uphold the vetoes of his party's President. His Goliath opposition, equipped with the powerful armor accumulated in 43 years of nearly uninterrupted rule, plus its growing disregard for national interest, even for personal civility, is described in shocking detail in THE FUTILE SYSTEM.

Getting the real inside view of what Congress has become—and Rhodes breaks with tradition to criticize his fellow Members only because the stakes for the country are so high—one wonders why he doesn't lay down his slingshot and go home, as more and more Congressmen are doing. He won't give up, however, for the same reason that he wrote this book. He feels if Americans learn that changes can be made only by changing the majority leadership, they will help him clean house and restore Congress to its former usefulness.

His faith in the people and in his own ability to give them the kind of Congress they want is so staunch that Minority Leader Rhodes says unabashedly: Send me the bodies who will elect me Speaker of the House, and I will put an end to THE FUTILE SYSTEM.

The Futile System

The Futile System

How to unchain Congress and
make the system work again

John J. Rhodes

EPM PUBLICATIONS, INC.

To all those who read this book,
with the hope that they will become disturbed enough to
take action toward a more responsive Congress.

Rhodes, John J.
  The futile system.
    1. United States. Congress—Reform. I. Title.
JK1061.R47   328.73   76–7926
ISBN 0–914440–17–9

EPM Publications, Inc., 1003 Turkey Run Road, McLean, Va. 22101
Printed in the United States of America

Design by Anne Hanger

Acknowledgments

The idea for THE FUTILE SYSTEM springs from the countless conversations I have had with Americans during my travels around the country as Minority Leader. Without the benefit of their views and perceptions of the legislative branch, this book could not have been written.

I am indebted to those Republican Members of the U.S. House of Representatives who were involved in the preparation of the Republican Legislative Agenda in 1975. The purpose of the Agenda and this book is similar: to give the people of the country a precise notion of what a Republican Congress would set out to accomplish.

For their special help, I would like to single out Representatives Robert McClory of Illinois, Clarence Brown of Ohio, and Bill Frenzel of Minnesota. They were kind enough to review portions of the manuscript and offer the considerable benefit of their respective expertise.

Among the many other individuals who graciously reviewed repeated drafts of this book with the aim of improving it, my thanks go to the staff of the Library of Congress, who checked for historical accuracy, and to Dr. Donald Wolfe of Loyola College, Baltimore, Maryland. Dr. Wolfe's invaluable insight is all the more appreciated in light of the fact that he is a loyal Democrat. It has been my goal from the beginning to write a book about the Democratic Congress in a language that can be understood not only by Republicans, but by Democrats and Independents as well. I am indebted to Dr. Wolfe for helping me towards that goal.

John J. Rhodes
Washington, D.C.

Contents

1   On the Outside Looking In

"A second flood, a simple famine, plagues of locusts everywhere. Or a catastrophic earthquake, I'd accept with some despair. But no, you sent us Congress. Good God, sir, was that fair?"
—John Adams, *from Sherman Edwards'*
Broadway musical "1776"

THE BELLS resound—two bells, loud and sharp—signaling that a vote has begun on the Floor of the United States House of Representatives. I am only vaguely aware of them. After 22 years in Congress, the ringing of the bells (two bells for a recorded vote, three bells for a quorum call, etc.) has become as much a part of life as breathing. Members respond to them naturally, effortlessly, almost unthinkingly, like Pavlov's dogs.

It takes a good five minutes, often longer, to reach the House Floor from one of the three House Office buildings. One of the good things about being Minority Leader is having an office in the Capitol. The proximity to the Floor enables me

1

to read and sign a few more letters and return a few more telephone calls before having to leave to vote.

My secretary sticks her head inside my office to inform me that there are two minutes remaining. I sign one more letter and slip out the rear door.

The trip from my office to the Floor is a quick one— between 45 seconds to a minute, depending on my pace.

I walk down a long narrow corridor. On the left is the conference room of the House International Relations Committee. On the right is the spiral staircase where the British soldiers entered the Capitol on the evening of August 24, 1814, the night they burned it.

Turning a corner, I enter Statuary Hall, formerly the House chamber. I pass a small brass plate located on the marble floor marking the spot where Abraham Lincoln had his desk in the 30th Congress. A few paces ahead lies a second brass plate marking the spot where John Quincy Adams suffered a fatal heart attack. The sixth President, who returned to Congress following his presidency, was carried into the Speaker's Room where he died two days later.

Beneath the watchful gaze of Will Rogers, immortalized in bronze (the famous humorist is said to have requested that his statue face the House Floor so that he could "keep an eye" on the Members), I pause momentarily to let a stream of visitors pass. They are on one of 120 Capitol tours that will take place this day.

The tourists having passed, I slip through a pair of large doors and onto the House Floor. The vote is on an amendment that I have decided to oppose. From my wallet I extract my voting card. It is roughly the size of a credit card. It bears my photograph and several punched holes, which is my personalized code. I insert the card into one of many electronic voting terminals affixed to the back of the seats and depress the button labeled "nay." A red light appears next to my name on the huge tote board above the press gallery.

I am about to leave the Floor when I notice a Republican

Member striding earnestly towards me.

He is James Hastings, a 4th-term Congressman from upstate New York. I had been in Jim's district a few days earlier to attend a fund-raising dinner held on his behalf and assume that he is coming over to thank me once again for making the trip.

"Hello John," he greets me. "Do you have a minute?"

We find a couple of unoccupied seats and sit down. "This may come as a shock, John, but I've decided to retire," he says.

It is a shock. Since I had been in his district the week before, I had naturally assumed that he was going all-out for re-election.

"You mean you're not going to run?" I ask incredulously.

"Right," he answers. "As a matter of fact, I'm going to quit Congress at the end of the month."

My initial surprise is compounded. There is always a list of incumbents who decide not to seek re-election. But it is very rare for a Member to step down before his term has expired.

Thinking that he may be in some political trouble back home, I ask, "Is everything all right?"

He assures me that everything is fine. "I've just had it," he explains. "I got tired, tired of being in the minority. We have to work twice as hard to be heard as those guys (he gestures towards the majority side) and I can't see things changing. I've simply had enough."

"You know what I mean, John," he adds, stating a point rather than asking a question.

I express to Hastings, who is one of the foremost authorities in the House on health legislation, my regret that he is leaving Congress. He tells me a little bit about the new job he will be taking with private industry. It sounds interesting. I wish him well and start back towards my office. Along the way, I think . . . about my friend Jim Hastings and his decision, and the heavy pressures faced by many of my other Republican colleagues.

Being in a congressional minority for a long period of time is depressing. To be sure, there is some solace to be derived from working to improve the program of the majority. Sometimes during a vote on a key amendment or an attempted veto override, the minority can band together to influence the outcome of events. But such cases are rare. For the most part, Members of the minority grow tired of being constantly against proposed bills and of never being able to enact anything of their own.

The prolonged period of time that Republicans have been in the minority in Congress has taken a hard toll on their spirit. Significantly, 17 Republican House Members chose retirement over re-election in 1974. Many of them represented safe districts and had no real fear of losing. They were simply tired of beating their heads against the wall, of having little direct legislative influence. They could see no hope for relief and as a result, Congress lost some truly able Members: Peter Frelinghuysen of New Jersey, Leslie Arends of Illinois, Howard Robison of New York, David Martin of Nebraska. The list does not stop there.

In addition to Jim Hastings of New York, Representatives Biester, Eshleman and Schneebeli of Pennsylvania, Gude of Maryland, Hutchinson of Michigan, Jarman of Oklahoma and Mosher of Ohio, all Republicans, have announced their intention to call it quits at the end of the 94th Congress. And the list will undoubtedly grow.

I fully understand the futility that comes from being locked into the minority. During my 22 years in Congress, all but two of these years—my freshman term—have been spent in the minority. Twenty years of having to be against things. As this is written, I am 59 years of age. I feel that I have several productive years ahead of me and can easily think of more useful ways to spend them than as a constant critic. Unless there is a significant change in Republican fortunes in the near future, my continued service in Congress is something I intend to review with great care. I know that many of my colleagues on the Republican side are of a similar frame of mind.

We have remained in Congress because the country needs a responsible minority as much as it needs a responsible and effective majority. It is our duty to do what we can to improve the legislative program put forth by the majority. When we are successful, we perform a useful service to the country.

There is a second responsibility of the minority. It is to try to become the nucleus of a new majority. There is always the hope that our political fortunes will improve in time, and it is this hope which gives us our real motivation.

Congress has changed greatly during my career. It has changed physically. When I arrived in 1953, there were two House office buildings. Today, there are three with a fourth being planned. In 1953, the Senators were all crowded into one office building. They now have two and are building a third.

Most everything in those days was done on a smaller scale. The staffs were smaller. The workload was smaller. The pressures were lighter. When I first started as a Congressman, I had a staff of five. Today, I employ a staff of 12 to handle my district-related business. During my first term, the House and Senate had a combined staff of 4,500 people and an operating budget of $42 million. Today, there are some 16,000 Capitol Hill employees and a budget of more than $414 million.

In the early days, I received an average of ten to twelve constituent letters a day. Now it is a rare day that I do not receive at least 150 letters from home. A typical session usually lasted until July or maybe early August. When the time arrived for Congress to adjourn, usually at the hottest point in the summer, my administrative assistant would pack up office supplies and files and we would all move back to Arizona for the remainder of the year. It was unusual for a Congressman to be able to afford a permanent district office in those days, so I would set up a makeshift office in some downtown Phoenix office building or anyplace where I could hold office hours. Today I have two permanent and fully staffed offices in my congressional district. Some Members have as many as four.

These are some of the physical changes. Congress has changed atmospherically as well.

A certain club atmosphere has long pervaded both Houses of Congress. This feeling of camaraderie among most of the Members comes from being engaged in a common task and having to face common pressures. It has—this spirit—always been an integral part of congressional life and has traditionally transcended party lines. In fact, some of the rules of Congress are specifically aimed at ensuring that Members treat each other with both courtesy and respect. While speaking on the Floor, for example, a Member is strictly prohibited by the rules from referring to another Member by name. He must refer instead to "the gentleman from Arizona" or "the distinguished gentleman." If one Member speaks ill of another Member on the Floor, the rules provide that a motion can be made for his remarks to be "stricken" from the *Record*. Outside of censure, having one's words stricken is the greatest rebuke a Member of Congress can receive.

When I was a young Congressman, I learned very quickly that one should never regard a political disagreement with another Member as a personal confrontation. Things just didn't work that way. I also learned that a good Member of Congress never, NEVER, loses his temper on the Floor. In the privacy of one's office or home, it is perfectly normal to rant and rave about the S.O.B. who did you in that day. But when you run into him the next day in a corridor or in the cloakroom, you treat him as though he is one of your best friends.

This spirit of congeniality and goodwill has helped the system work for the benefit of the people. In years past, Members went out of their way to help a colleague in need, even if the colleague belonged to the other party. When I was a member of the Appropriations Committee, it was not at all unusual for a Member to request my assistance in obtaining financing for a project in his district. If the project had merit, I usually did whatever I could to accommodate him. And if for some reason I couldn't help him, he almost always understood.

Members of Congress still strive to help one another, but not nearly to the extent that they once did. And Members still treat each other with civility, but not anywhere near the civility of earlier days. Congress has changed. Of this there can be no question.

The atmosphere in and around Congress today is far more acrid than at any time during my career. The Members are louder, more uptight, hostile and devious. The average Congressman has always been partisan, but never so partisan as he is today. Today's Members—particularly many of the newer Members—have failed to master the art of disagreeing without being disagreeable.

It is certainly not my intention to hand down a blanket indictment of the entire membership of Congress. After all, there are 535 individual Members, many of whom are conscientious, hard working, intelligent and unselfish. I am speaking only in terms of broad trends and averages, with the hope that things may yet change for the better.

The average Congressman of yesteryear was congenial, polite and willing to work with his colleagues whenever possible. Most important, his main concern was attending to his congressional duties. Today, a large number of Congressmen are cynical, abrasive, frequently uncommunicative and ambitious to an inordinate degree. In their eagerness to draw attention to themselves—and advance politically—they frustrate the legislative process.

Representative William Hungate, a Democrat from Missouri, spoke of the changes when he announced his decision to retire at the end of the 94th Congress: "Where once criticism fell without impact, it now lands heavily. Where once exorbitant demands aroused little feeling, they now provoke annoyance. I have found that since I entered office the duties have increased dramatically, exceeded only by public dissatisfaction with the Congress."

Craig Hosmer, a Republican Representative from California who retired in 1973, put it even more bluntly: "Congress just isn't fun anymore."

No one expects the legislative process to be fun. But it certainly doesn't have to be as grim as it now is.

I recall an incident illustrating the new abrasive breed that took place at the 1972 Republican Convention. I was chairman of the Platform Committee and had decided before the Convention that any citizen who wished to testify was entitled to do so. Because of the time factor, however, it was necessary for me to appoint seven subcommittees in order to give everyone a chance to be heard. I decided to budget the time in such a way as to enable the full Platform Committee to hear testimony from at least one prominent spokesman for each side of each major issue. All other individuals who desired to testify could do so before the appropriate subcommittee. This seemed to me to be the most practical and fair way for the Platform Committee to operate, and most everyone seemed satisfied with the arrangements I had made. Congressman Donald Riegle was a notable exception.

Don Riegle was at the time a Republican Member of the House from Michigan with strong views on the ideological direction of the Republican Party. He approached me one afternoon and asked if he could testify on the general subject of the party's future. I explained the way that I had budgeted the available time and told him that I would be pleased to arrange for him to testify before one of the subcommittees.

"I don't want to testify before one of the subcommittees," he answered. "I want to testify before the full committee."

Once again I explained that two individuals, one a conservative and the other a liberal, had been previously chosen to testify before the full Platform Committee on the future of the Party. There was simply no more time available.

"You won't let me testify because I'm a liberal," Don complained.

"Don," I said to him, "you're a great liberal. But there's an even greater liberal in our party. His name is Jack Javits and he is the one that will testify before the full committee!"

"Don't worry," Riegle replied, "I'll get more time on television than you will anyway." With that, he promptly called a press conference to denounce the Platform Committee as a complete sham and its chairman as a tyrant.

Riegle was absolutely correct in his statement that he could command more media time than I. When he arrived in Washington in 1966, he was one of the darlings of the national media. Why? Because he was different. He was an outspoken liberal, a maverick, in a party whose mainstream is located somewhere to the right of center. Whenever Riegle made a statement, because of who he was and where he was, it was instant news. In 1973 Riegle decided to switch parties and become a Democrat. Since then he has rarely been heard from. He receives very little in the way of national press coverage now because in the mainly liberal Democratic Party, he is just one of many. Riegle is a maverick no more.

Otis Pike of New York is another attention-getter who seems to have submerged his legislative responsibility for the sake of self-aggrandizement.

Pike was chosen to serve as chairman of a Select Intelligence Committee set up in the summer of 1975. The committee's mandate was to look into allegations of improper activities undertaken mainly by the Central Intelligence Agency. It was important that these allegations, which had surfaced during the Watergate and impeachment hearings, be pursued. Congress and the people are entitled to know what is being done by intelligence-gathering agencies in the name of the United States Government. At the same time, the committee was traversing sensitive ground. America needs a viable intelligence apparatus and selective leaks could easily weaken our covert intelligence capabilities. It was critical that the members of the committee, particularly the chairman, proceed with discretion and taste.

Much to the surprise of his friends, Otis Pike became the antithesis of both qualities. He must have envisioned himself as the Peter Rodino of 1976, presiding over a full-blown televised investigation of the horrors committed by the U.S. intelligence community. It was well-known that he had serious senatorial aspirations and it became obvious that he regarded his chairmanship as a potentially effective political launching pad.

The major source of conflict between Chairman Pike and the Ford Administration centered around committee access to highly classified information. No one in the Administration doubted the right of elected Members of Congress to examine top-secret documents. What was doubted was the wisdom of constantly having those documents appear in *The New York Times* or broadcast over CBS News. President Ford had been understandably outraged by committee leaks of sensitive material related to the 1973 Egyptian-Israeli War that were damaging to our relationship with both Egypt and Israel. The President did not want a recurrence of such irresponsibility.

Pike used his forum as chairman to denounce the President's reluctance to turn over *carte blanche* highly classified materials. He directed his committee to issue three separate resolutions citing Secretary of State Henry Kissinger, keeper of most of the desired material, for contempt of Congress. So tenuous were the grounds upon which the citations were based that the committee was finally forced to withdraw them. That they were issued at all illustrates the rabid desire of the chairman to force a confrontation on the House Floor.

Mainly in response to the urgings of House Republicans, President Ford agreed to grant the Pike Committee the documents it sought provided that he could have the power of final clearance over public release of the committee report. Chair-

WASHINGTON CONFIDENTIAL

man Pike agreed to the arrangement.

What followed was an unconscionable series of damaging leaks that undercut the effectiveness of our intelligence operations and endangered the lives of many of our foreign agents around the world. No effort was made by the chairman to plug the leaks. If anything, his arrogant rhetoric increased.

In January, 1976, the Pike Committee, including the chairman, voted to release the final report, despite the fact that the report contained some 200 items which the Administration considered to be highly classified. President Ford had thought he had a gentlemen's agreement with Otis Pike but what he got instead were charges of perpetrating a cover-up akin to Watergate.

So blatant was the arrogant breach of faith committed by Pike that the full House voted to block the release of his committee's report. It is exceedingly rare that a committee of Congress is formally rebuked or overruled by the full membership. Otis Pike had simply gone too far.

Another Member whose legislative compass has gone awry is Senator Henry "Scoop" Jackson. Few Members of Congress of either party doubt Jackson's intelligence and his natural ability as a legislator; even fewer doubt his ambition. Scoop's main problem in Congress is very simple. He wants to be President. He wants to be President so much that he seems to care little about what effect his statements and actions may have on the legislative process as well as on our international standing.

Consider Jackson's ill-starred efforts to help Soviet Jews get out of the U.S.S.R. The Jackson-Vanik amendment, attached to a trade bill passed in December 1974, required the Soviet Union to allow freer emigration of Soviet Jews in order to qualify for trade benefits. Popular with the American Jewish community, the amendment was ostensibly designed to help lift a repressive Soviet policy. It had a decidedly opposite effect.

According to State Department figures, in 1973, before the Jackson-Vanik amendment, 33,500 Soviet Jews were allowed to emigrate. In 1975, after Jackson-Vanik was enacted, the number of emigrating Jews fell to 12,000; this is proof again that Congress only makes a problem worse when it tries to force other countries of the world into a policy position against their will.

Senator Jackson's rabid presidential ambitions have definitely impaired his effectiveness as a Member of Congress. They have also impaired the effectiveness of other Members, as well as the entire legislative process. Senator James Abourezk, a Democratic member of the Senate Interior Committee which is chaired by Jackson, bluntly charged his chairman with "using the committee to run for President."

"In hearings," said Abourezk, "the issues are taken not in terms of what ought to be done but in terms of what's good for Scoop's campaign."

Abourezk is the knowledgeable chairman of the Senate Interior Committee's subcommittee on Indian Affairs who grew up on an Indian reservation himself. Early in 1975, his subcommittee held a series of very important hearings on the various health-related problems confronting the American Indian community. The health services which are made available to American Indians were investigated and some highly pertinent and previously unknown facts were uncovered. Impressed with the information developed by the Abourezk subcommittee, one television network decided to produce a news documentary on the subject. The network arranged to film the subcommittee at work during one of its morning sessions.

On the day the filming was to take place, Abourezk arrived at the hearing room and discovered that his nameplate had been removed. Behind the new nameplate and seated in his chair was Senator Jackson. Smiling broadly, Jackson explained that the issue of Indian health care was so important that it deserved the attention of the full Interior Committee. The filming took place as planned, except that Jackson was the star of the show. As soon as the television cameras left the room so did Scoop, and the remainder of the work fell once again to the Abourezk subcommittee.

What can be done to ensure that Congress is made up of individuals whose principal interest is legislation and not reaching some other office? Closer scrutiny by the voters is one obvious answer. When evaluating a candidate for the House or Senate, the voters should demand to know his or her opinions regarding issues that Congress can affect. They should also demand that he possess a working knowledge of the legislative process. It is surprising how many Members really do not understand even the basics of the system. I had a freshman Member, a bright young rising star, come up to me on the Floor during one of the opening days of a recent session and ask, "Just how many Members are there in this body?"

It is such basic ignorance that leads me to conclude that many Members run for Congress not because they have any great interest in legislation, but because of the opportunities for future advancement that service in Congress presents. They are here because they enjoy the publicity that comes from being a Member and because there is always the possibility of a higher office opening up for them. As far as the day-to-day business of being a legislator is concerned, too many of them couldn't care less.

My proposal for dealing with this problem is to prohibit Members of Congress from seeking the presidency or vice-presidency until two years after the end of his or her congressional term. An exception would be made when an unforeseen vacancy in the presidency or vice-presidency occurs, in which case the 25th Amendment would apply. Such a two-year moratorium would mean that no Congressman or Senator could run a national campaign—or engage in the type of preliminary politicking that precedes a national campaign—while serving in Congress. Such a proviso would have two effects: First, overly-ambitious Members would not be distracted from legislative business. Second, individuals whose true motivation from the beginning was to run for President would be dissuaded from running for Congress. The end result would be that Congress would be made up of men and women whose interest and focus of attention is worthwhile legislation.

Eliminating the over-ambitiousness and partisan rhetoric of individual Congressmen is but one step towards a revitalization of the legislative branch. The switching of party control of Congress is an even more important step. For nearly 40 years Congress has been run by Democrats; in the House, we have had nearly 40 years of Democratic Speakers and Democratic committee chairmen. All of the power and influence available to the legislative branch has rested exclusively in the hands of one party, with no effective check or balance. As a result, the all-important committee structure has become atrophied through age. Old problems increase in complexity and new problems emerge, yet Congress continues to do its business in the same old way. Why? Because people in power are reluctant to tamper with a system that has served them and their predecessors well over the years. Under no real pressure to be responsive to public opinion—because the people have clearly demonstrated that they do not punish poor congressional performance—Members of the majority leadership have grown fat and lazy. The majority of congressional actions are aimed not at producing results for the American people as much as at perpetuating the longevity and comfort of the men who run Congress. It is a rip-off of the American taxpayer, injurious to the national interest and an insult to the dignity of the legislative branch envisioned by the founding fathers. The massive deterioration that has taken place within the U.S. Congress during the past two decades is more than just a pity; it poses serious questions for the future of the country. For unless "the people's branch" can be reformed—and soon—it is unlikely that America will find herself able to meet the pressing challenges that lie ahead.

Had the party roles been reversed and the Republicans been

in power for 39 out of the last 43 years, the same legislative deterioration would have occurred. People who are in power for too long, without any check on their power, inevitably become either arrogant or listless or both. My party would have surely fallen prey to the same natural forces.

As a matter of fact, the evidence suggests that it once did. From 1895 through 1910, a period of 16 years, the House was controlled by Republicans. The powers accumulated by Speaker Joe Cannon, and before him Speaker Thomas "Czar" Reed, were so great that immediately following the takeover by the Democrats in 1911, several major rules were instituted to reduce the Speaker's power.

Although the current House Speaker, Carl Albert of Oklahoma, is certainly no "Czar" Reed or Cannon, his brand of leadership is weak, inefficient and unresponsive to national problems. The men who currently run Congress are out of touch with the American people, unaware and unheeding of their needs and priorities. They are mostly incapable of acting effectively on key issues because they are more concerned with internal politics than the public interest. Their party has been in power too long.

More than anything else, Congress needs to have its windows opened to let in some fresh air. Changing the individual faces of the majority rank and file won't work. Congress cannot be changed until the people at the top, the people who make up the majority leadership, are changed. The only sure way to change the majority leadership is to change party control of Congress. Only when the people are willing to change party control—to elect more individual Republicans than Democrats—can Congress cease being a public joke, an object of universal ridicule, and start conducting the public business.

It is a prospect that I look forward to eagerly.

2   The Congress Nobody Knows

"Power has to be insecure to be responsive. It's got to have something to lose. And the definition of perfect tyranny is an institution that really has nothing to lose."

—Ralph Nader

IT HAS BEEN obvious to me for some time that many teachers of civics and government in our schools must be doing a poor job of teaching the fundamentals of the legislative process. "This is Congress," they will explain to their pupils. "It has two parts: A House of Representatives and a Senate. Bills are introduced by Members of Congress, sent to a committee and reported to the Floor. The Members vote on bills and send them to the President. If the President signs them, the bills become law." End of lesson. This simplistic approach has led to a shockingly high degree of governmental illiteracy among the American population.

But it would be unfair and wrong to place the entire blame

'What a fantastic new idea!'

for the lack of public understanding of Congress on teachers. The truth is that Members of Congress themselves do a pretty good job of obscuring the record so that the people remain in the dark.

A member of Congress can manipulate his public image at will. It is characteristic of human nature that people tend to see in others what they want to see. For instance, the current vogue in Congress is to be for "fiscal responsibility" and against "big Government". Republicans have been preaching this doctrine for many years. Only recently, however, as the size of the federal budget has ballooned, have the American people become receptive to the phrases. Now, even liberal Democrats, who were most responsible for the incredible growth of the federal bureaucracy, are talking the fiscal conservative line.

The liberal Democrats go home to their constituents and deliver an impassioned "let's hold the line against big Government spending" speech, or send out a district-wide newsletter lamenting the most recent rise in inflation and espousing the need for effective budget control, and then proceed to vote for just about every new and expensive program that comes before Congress. One of the oldest tricks in the game is for a Member who is worried that he may be tagged in the next election as a big spender to refuse to vote to raise the ceiling on the federal debt. He votes for all the big spending bills and then refuses to raise the debt to enable the Government to meet its obligations! Then he goes back to his district and says, "See, I'm a fiscal conservative. I voted against raising the debt ceiling." It is pure sham. But it never ceases to amaze me how many liberal Democrats get away with the hoax year after year.

I can't begin to recall the many times I've had a businessman tell me, in reference to some Member of Congress, "You know, I always thought he was a flaming liberal, but he gave us a speech the other day that was as conservative as any I've heard."

What happened was that the Congressman had simply dusted off his standard "Chamber of Commerce Speech," in which he accentuates his pro-business side and ignores completely the votes he has cast that are decidely anti-business. It is a con game at which Members of Congress are remarkably adept.

Even the *Congressional Record,* the official transcript of all that transpires on the Floor of both the House and Senate, can be altered by a Member concerned with his public image. Whenever a Member rises to speak during Floor debate, he routinely requests of the chair that he be given unanimous consent to revise and extend his remarks. Usually within an hour after he has finished speaking, one of the clerks will hand him a roughly typed transcript of his remarks which he is free to amend in any way he wants. Most of a Member's changes are merely grammatical because extemporaneous remarks frequently lack the precision of the written word. Once in a while a Member may direct his legislative assistant to incorporate into the text of his remarks some additional facts or figures which he may not have had in front of him during his speech. There is certainly nothing wrong with making changes of this kind. After all, a Member who polishes up his language is actually performing a service for those who will read the *Record* later on. Similarly, a Member who extends his remarks subsequent to their delivery is doing a service for his colleagues who must endure many long hours of Floor debate.

Unfortunately, however, the power to alter the *Congressional Record* is badly abused by some Members. They use this power not to add to the quality of the Floor debate but to give a distorted impression of their own roles. It is not at all uncommon, for instance, for a Member to seek the recognition of the chair to request that his remarks appear in the *Record* at a strategic point in the debate, and thus it appears that he participated in the debate when in fact he did not.

Such a maneuver is self-serving in that a Member may

appear to have taken on one of the managers of a Floor debate by making all sorts of charges that go unanswered because they were never actually spoken. It can also have deleterious effects on legislation before Congress. During debate on an important piece of labor legislation in 1971 for example, Democratic Congresswoman Edith Green of Oregon inserted a charge into the *Record* that a substitute bill offered by Republican John Erlenborn of Illinois would require repeal of the Equal Pay for Equal Work Act. Obviously, there was no response from the author of the bill because Mrs. Green's remarks were not actually spoken. Yet Labor Department officials who read the *Record* the next day, took Erlenborn's "silence" as an indication that Mrs. Green's charge was correct. They promptly put the word out that the Erlenborn substitute was unacceptable. In truth, Mrs. Green was incorrect in her charge but it was too late to correct the damage and the substitute was substantially altered in Conference.

Even more distressing to those who place a high premium on accuracy is the power that Members may exercise to delete Floor remarks which might hurt their image back home. During debate on a controversial pay raise for Members of Congress, for example, House Administration Committee Chairman Wayne Hays, a tough-talking Ohio Democrat, had a spirited exchange with freshman Republican Millicent Fenwick of New Jersey. The high point in the exchange occurred when Hays threatened to cut off the staff allowances of Republicans who objected to the pay raise. "I think," Mrs. Fenwick said softly, "that we have heard something here today for which we are all going to be sorry and ashamed."

The next day there was not the slightest trace of Congressman Hays' remarks in the *Record*. He obviously felt after sober reflection that the harsh admonishment he had directed towards Mrs. Fenwick would further damage his already crusty public image and therefore ordered his words deleted from the *Record* altogether.

A really conscientious citizen may go to the trouble of

researching a Member's voting record before election day. Yet even a Member's voting record, the most visible evidence of his philosophy, is frequently a misleading account of his actual actions in Congress. That is because there are numerous ways for a Congressman to influence the outcome of legislation before the vote on final passage ever takes place.

It is not uncommon, for example, for a Member of Congress to vote according to public opinion in his district on the final passage of a bill even though he may have voted in a completely opposite direction in committee or during the critically important amendment process on the Floor. The Member knows that his vote on final passage is the one most likely to receive attention back home. His previous votes, often beyond public view, are likely to be unknown. But they may have been far more important than his vote on final passage.

There are always a good number of House Members who respond to party Whip counts by saying, "It will really hurt me in my district to have to vote with you on this one, but if you need me to win I'll try to help." On key votes, these Members can frequently represent the critical margin between victory and defeat. They usually stand towards the rear of the chamber during the voting and hold back their votes until the last possible moment. If the leadership calculates during the closing minute of voting that it already has the votes to win, the undecideds are released to "vote their district." If on the other hand, it is determined that their votes are needed, the signal goes out and most of them will risk temporary disfavor back home for the sake of party unity.

Once a vote has been concluded, Members have the opportunity to change their votes by standing in the well and seeking the recognition of the Tally Clerk. For example, if a Member voted with his leadership against the majority of opinion in his district and realized subsequently that the final outcome would not be affected by his individual vote, he may proceed to the well to correct the official record. If he wants to change his vote from yes to no, he will so instruct the

Clerk, who will then announce: "Mr. Jones: Off aye, on no, for Mr. Jones."

By exercising his power to change his vote, a Member of Congress may have the best of both worlds: he can stick with his leadership during the vote and then change the record to satisfy his constituents after the vote has been concluded.

A Member's ability to change both the *Congressional Record* and his voting record makes it genuinely difficult to obtain a truly accurate picture of what a Member of Congress stands for and what he actually does in Washington. The facts are there for the determined digger, but the average citizen has neither the time nor the inclination to conduct such an exhaustive search. So the great farce goes on.

Most Americans don't understand that Congress is run by the leadership of the majority party. In the next chapter, I describe its important powers. It is the leadership of the majority party that determines what Congress does and whether Congress will be active or passive, liberal or conservative. Because it doesn't have the votes, the minority has no positive power. Its chief influence is negative. The current Republican minority, for example, has had some success in sustaining presidential vetoes, but that is because there happens to be a Republican President. A Democratic President presumably would not be vetoing many bills from a Democratic Congress and in that case, the Republican minority would be mainly cut out of the legislative equation.

Congress is an institution. However, Americans are unfortunately and unreasonably conditioned to viewing politics and government from the perspective of the individual. If one wanted to evaluate the effectiveness of a huge corporation, one would naturally want to see the books, the productivity records, and the entire overview of the firm. Corporation personnel would be considered but only after the institutional machinery had been thoroughly examined. The individuals involved are important because they are responsible for ensuring the maximum effectiveness of the machinery. Yet it is the viability of the machinery itself that determines the success or failure of the corporation.

But the American people do not recognize Congress as an institution. Instead, they tend to concentrate their attention on the individual Member who represents them, a failing I call the "good old Congressman Joe" syndrome. When asked, an overwhelming majority of Americans condemn the performance of Congress as a whole, but they maintain a generally high regard for their individual Congressmen.

"Congress is doing a terrible job," a voter says. "But not our good old Joe," he adds in the next breath. "Good old Joe has the right ideas. It's those other guys who must be messing things up."

Due to the chronic public ignorance of Congress as an institution, Members find it very easy to escape the consequences of Congress' poor track record. As Congressman Les Aspin, a Democrat from Wisconsin put it: "I don't care what my district thinks of Congress as long as 51% of it likes me." [1]

The irony of a Member of the Democratic majority going back to his district and scoring political brownie points by attacking Congress drives me up the wall. After all, it is his party that runs Congress! His vote at the start of the session helped elect the majority leadership that controls every significant aspect of legislative activity. Yet he has the gall to absolve himself from any blame for Congress' inability to act on the issues. If he isn't to blame, who is?

What has happened is simultaneously fascinating and frightening: Congress is not being held to account by the American people. This is in marked contrast with the Executive. Every four years, the voters consciously elect a President. The party that has controlled the White House during the previous four years is invariably held accountable for its past performance, as it should be. Two recent Presidents, Harry Truman and Lyndon Johnson, chose not to seek re-election as a result of public displeasure with their policies. More recently, President Nixon was forced to resign because of his role in the Watergate cover-up. In all of these cases, the President was held directly accountable for policies and activities undertaken during his term of office.

Yet the legislative branch answers to no one. It fails to do the job and the people know it, yet the same party leadership remains securely in power. Congressional unaccountability is one of the great paradoxes of our time and for me, it is the main reason for the futility of the system.

The people do not understand that the majority party in Congress controls everything of significance that Congress does. Moreover, I sometimes wonder if many Americans actually know which political party is in the majority in Congress?

The Democrats have controlled Congress for 22 consecutive years and 39 out of the last 43 years. Only in 1947-48, when the country was completely fed up with World War II price controls, and in 1953-54, when Dwight Eisenhower's immense popularity helped sweep Republican candidates into office, have Republicans controlled both houses of Congress.

Sometimes I think that Democratic dominance of the legislative branch of Government has been one of the best kept secrets of the century. When people visualize the federal Government, what most of them see is not the Congress but the most visible individual in Washington: the President of the United States. The President is a Republican and therefore many people believe that Congress must be Republican too.

Consider this letter I received from a distraught lady in Sun City Arizona, written April 11, 1975, the day after President Ford's Foreign Policy Address to Congress. The event was marred by the immature behavior of some Democratic Members who decided to walk out of the chamber while the President was still speaking. Unfortunately, the television cameras recorded their departure and the lady from Arizona was very upset.

> I was never so shocked as I was last night when I saw those Democrats walk out on our President. I hold you responsible for this and am ashamed of you as an Arizonan. I would have expected the Minority Leader to have more control over the members of his own party.

Or the following letter from a businessman in Tampa, Florida.

> Every time I turn around I have to fill out another form. I am only a small businessman trying to earn a living but have had to employ a clerk to do nothing but fill out your damned forms. Business is being regulated to death!
>
> You Republicans have been in power for a long time. When are you going to do something about this?

Both of these citizens have confused the Congress with the Executive. Another example of this common mistake is the fact that the high budget deficits of recent years are often attributed to the Executive. President Ford has been severely criticized for having accepted a budget deficit of $80 billion in fiscal year 1977. This criticism is misdirected. The Constitution is explicit that Congress shall control the nation's purse strings. No President can spend a dime that hasn't first been appropriated by Congress. A President's budget is supposed to represent a realistic estimate of what will be spent, given the existing programs. The President is not supposed to engage in wishful thinking at budget time.

In fact, with enactment of the Budget and Impoundment Control Act of 1974, Congress effectively demanded that a President strictly adhere to the established budget. The law provides among other things that a President must spend every dime Congress appropriates. Were a President to impound (hold back) appropriated funds, as many have, he would violate the law.

I remember what Lyndon Johnson, one of the shrewdest politicians in modern American history, used to do as President. He would take items out of his budget such as the school lunch program knowing full well that Congress would restore them. Then he could claim that his budget was lower than the one finally enacted by Congress. He realized that most people blame the Executive, albeit incorrectly, for the size of the federal budget.

People also blame the Executive for the bureaucratic tendencies of the regulatory agencies whereas, in fact, Congress should take the blame. In the first place, all of the agencies were set up by laws passed by Congress. And if the agencies have promulgated policies and regulations that harass the citizenry, it is Congress that should be held accountable for failing to exercise "oversight" of its laws. Oversight is what we call the congressional activity of looking back at all of the laws previously enacted to see if they are working properly. Of course, it is universally conceded that the Democratic Congresses of the past have ignored their oversight function. It is a subject to which I return in a later chapter.

Before I discuss some of my specific complaints about recent Democratic Congresses, as well as some of the specific changes a Republican Congress would make in the system, I want to give you a look into the innermost power sanctums of the majority leadership. Here you will see some of the men who really run Congress. When Congress performs well, it is they and their party who deserve most of the credit. When Congress does not perform well, it is they and their party who should be held responsible.

3   The Power Barons

"Majorities without discipline are not majorities"
> —Senate Majority Leader Mike Mansfield

ALMOST every book about Congress that I have seen contains a description of "How a bill becomes a law." Many of these descriptions go into considerable detail and some of them do an excellent job of explaining the legislative process. However, they usually neglect to mention an important point. It is this: the majority leadership controls the legislative machinery through which a bill must pass in order to become law. Each Member of Congress has one vote, but the power of the majority leadership is such that the individual's vote often counts for very little.

Leadership needs to be defined. By leadership I do not mean the ability to inspire, such as the delivery of a stirring speech by an individual Member of Congress or a stunning performance on television or radio.

My use of the term leadership here means the elected leaders of the majority party in Congress. In the House of Representatives, the top leadership includes the Speaker, the Majority Leader, the Whip, and the Chairman of the majority Caucus. It is they who are supposed to make the legislative process work.

The majority leadership also includes the chairmen of the standing committees. These chairmen are all members of the majority party and exercise great influence in the legislative process. A committee chairman can actually keep the entire Congress from working its will, even when a majority of his own party favors action. There are examples in the following chapter.

The committee chairmen, who are mainly selected because of their length of service on the committee, are power brokers in their own right and can do almost anything they please. Representative Philip Campbell of Kansas, a former chairman of the House Rules Committee, once told his colleagues:

> You can go to hell. It makes no difference what a majority of you decide. If it meets with my disapproval, it shall not be done. I am the committee. In me reposes absolute obstructive power.[2]

I have selected the four top members of the majority leadership in the House and two House committee chairmen as subjects for closer study. I know all of these individuals well. I regard them as personal friends. My purpose is not to question either their motives or intelligence. My purpose is to identify them as individuals whose misfortune it has been to preside over a majority that has controlled Congress for an unhealthy period of time . . . a majority that is largely oblivious to the pressing need for congressional change and reform as well as to the real needs and desires of the American people.

The Leaders

THE SPEAKER: Carl Bert Albert, age 67, is the 46th Speaker of the U.S. House of Representatives. Affectionately dubbed "the little giant from little Dixie," he worked his way up the leadership ladder of the Democratic Party in the House, assuming the Speakership in 1971 upon the retirement of John Mc-Cormack of Massachusetts.

Speaker Albert, a Rhodes scholar, is an intelligent man who is very fair in his dealings with all Members of the House as individuals. He is keenly aware of the hazards involved in presiding over a large majority and goes to exceptional lengths not to offend any of the various Democratic factions.

The Speaker's mode of operation is best described by a statement he has made often in my presence: "I never do anything without the consent of my committee chairmen." This attitude is not without its virtue. Yet it has frequently brought utter chaos to the Floor and caused great delay in the passage of key legislation. Why? Because jurisdictional disputes frequently arise between committees. The disputes over energy provide good examples. In the House alone, there are 14 committees and 27 subcommittees that claim jurisdiction over some phase of the Energy Research and Development Administration. Committee chairmen and key subcommittee chairmen have jockeyed for the inside track on energy since it became a big national issue. With so many cooks in the congressional kitchen, is it any wonder that action has been so slow in coming?

Energy is not the only area in which conflict between committees has stood in the way of legislative progress. The constant battles between the Ways and Means Committee and Interstate and Foreign Commerce Committee for control over health legislation come to mind, as do the battles between Interstate and Foreign Commerce and the Committee on Education and Labor over certain education bills.

Obviously, there is need for strong leadership. But Speaker Albert's insistence that he operate with the complete concurrence of his chairmen stands in the way. He has found it impossible to persuade stubborn and jealous chairmen to work together and get something done. His virtue, of desiring com-

CARL ALBERT
FRESHMAN
PUPPY
OBEDIENCE
SCHOOL

'THIS WHOLE THING IS IMPOSSIBLE!!'

VETO!
VETO!

plete consensus before making any move, is virtue in excess.

The Speaker's leadership has come under attack from various quarters. In June, 1975, a group of freshman Democrats had a well-publicized meeting with him in order to voice their complaints about the quality of the majority leadership. One of the freshmen, Congressman Robert Carr of Michigan, declared at the time: "The leadership is out of touch with Congress, and Congress is out of touch with the country. The (Democratic) leadership is still trying to find 1935 answers to 1975 problems."

There has been considerable speculation that Speaker Albert may retire at the end of the current term.*This speculation was initially given credibility when Congressman Richard Bolling of Missouri, a close personal friend of the Speaker, announced his intention to run for Majority Leader if the Speaker steps down. Were Albert to retire, an intensive power struggle among House Democrats would follow. It is generally felt that the Speakership—given another Democratic Congress— probably would go to House Majority Leader O'Neill. However, there may be considerable jockeying for all of the leadership jobs, including the Speakership.

If Speaker Albert does seek another term, it is doubtful that there would be a serious attempt to take away his power. Congressional Democrats have a history of graceful leadership transitions, in interesting contrast to Republicans. Our leadership struggles in Congress have traditionally been intense and often bloody.

THE MAJORITY LEADER: Thomas P. O'Neill, Jr. is easily one of the most affable men I know. A big bear of a man, Tip is a Boston Irish politician of the old school, a character right out of Edwin O'Connor's *The Last Hurrah*. He is known for his ready grin, friendly slaps on the back and humorous political stories. He is great fun to be around at a social occasion.

He is also the most partisan man I have ever known—so partisan that for him the word Republican is a red flag waved

* Several weeks after this book was published, Speaker Albert announced that he would not be a candidate for re-election in 1976.

beneath the nose of a feisty bull. In contrast to Speaker Albert, who maintains a fair-minded approach towards all Members regardless of party, Tip can be impossible to deal with if you are in the minority. There is nothing in the rules of the House that requires the Majority Leader to consult with the minority leadership on the scheduling of legislation, recesses, and the like. Yet most past majority leaders have done so believing that the interests of the whole Congress are served by a degree of inter-party cooperation. But not Tip. "The people gave us the mandate," he has declared, "and we're not going to give it up."

On another occasion, Tip announced: "Republicans are just going to have to get it through their heads that they are not going to write legislation!"

Still, we try. At the start of the 94th Congress, in January, 1974, I proposed what I call a "consensus government" to avoid stalemates between the Congress and the Executive. I called upon the majority leadership in Congress to come together with the minority leadership and the President to determine areas of mutual agreement. Items of agreement could be identified at once and areas of disagreement simply set aside for future debate.

My consensus proposal never had a chance to work because Tip O'Neill would not let it work. He would much rather stand up on the Floor and deliver a partisan attack on the President for vetoing a bill than sit down with the President early in the legislative process to help avoid a veto. Throughout 1975, Tip began almost every session with a brief harangue against Administration policy. I have included several memorable examples, along with my replies, in the Appendix.

As keeper of the legislative calendar, the Majority Leader has a powerful timing advantage when it comes to enacting the majority program. The Majority Leader schedules bills to suit his own purposes. He can place a controversial bill on the calendar with little prior notice and thus take the opposition by surprise. Or, if his Whip check reveals that the opposition is well-organized, he can pull a bill off the calendar at the last moment in order to give his side time to marshal a sufficient number of votes. The presidentially vetoed strip mining bill, for example, was taken off the House calendar when the majority leadership determined that it was lacking the votes to override.

Towards the end of each week, it is the duty of the Majority Leader to rise on the Floor and announce the legislative calendar for the coming week. It is a very important event, for Members of both parties base their travel schedules on the information put out by the Majority Leader. Few things disturb Members more than some last-minute change in the legislative schedule because it presents them with the painful choice of either cancelling an important engagement in their district or missing a crucial vote.

The high degree of precision required in the planning of the weekly legislative schedule has been lacking in the majority leadership. The haphazard manner in which the schedule is arranged—resulting in sessions that last well into the night on some days and only an hour or two on other days—is a source of pique among both Republicans and Democrats.

As Minority Leader, I am expected to advise Members on my side of the aisle about the legislative business before Congress. Since I have no control over the schedule, the only way I have to familiarize myself with the anticipated workload is to ask the Majority Leader. What follows is an example from the *Record* of the routine type of exchange that I have with Majority Leader O'Neill concerning the legislative program. It illustrates the confusion prevalent on the majority side.

MR. RHODES: Mr. Speaker, I take this time to inquire of the distinguished majority leader as to the program for the balance of the day and the week, and any other information on this subject which he can make available to us.

MR. O'NEILL: Mr. Speaker, if the distinguished minority leader will be kind enough to yield, I will be happy to respond to him and give the program for the remainder of this week.

MR. RHODES: I yield to the distinguished majority leader.

MR. O'NEILL: Mr. Speaker, the program for the rest of the day is as follows:

The next item is H.R. 3474, Energy Research and Development Authorization. That is ERDA.

We would hope that we would be able to finish this legislation today, but I understand there is an amendment of controversy in the ERDA bill. Consequently, it is the intent of the committee to rise at 6:30. If we do not finish ERDA today, we will have it first on the schedule for tomorrow.

The next item we had scheduled was H.R. 49, petroleum reserves, Elk Hills. That will be put over until Monday. H.R. 7500, State Department authorization, will be put over until Monday. H.R. 5884, International Economic Policy Act, will be scheduled for tomorrow.

MR. RHODES: Mr. Speaker, it is my understanding that the Elk Hills bill would come up on Tuesday rather than Monday.

MR. O'NEILL: As I understand, there has been an agreement by all parties concerned. The only one I have spoken to on the other side is the gentleman from California (Mr. Bell) and it is my understanding that both the Armed Services Committee and the committee chaired by the gentleman from Montana (Mr. Melcher) were in agreement to bring it up on Monday.

MR. RHODES: My understanding from members of the Committee on Interior and Insular Affairs is that they desire the matter to come up on Tuesday.

MR. O'NEILL: That has been discussed, but I thought an agreement on Tuesday had been reached.

MR. RHODES: Could the distinguished majority leader tell the House approximately how long we will be in session tomorrow?

MR. O'NEILL: I would ask unanimous consent that when the House adjourn tonight it adjourn to meet tomorrow at 10 o'clock.

MR. RHODES: With what understanding?

MR. O'NEILL: Then we would follow the will of the Members of the House as to what time they want to finish the business tomorrow. We do not intend to set a specific hour.

MR. RHODES: I had conversations with several of the leadership on the gentleman's side of the aisle, and I am a little amazed, because the conversation led me to believe that it was fairly firm that the House would adjourn tomorrow some time between 4 or 4:30. Is that not the situation?

MR. O'NEILL: No; that is not so. But the gentleman knows that is the way things are. One hears one thing from my side, and I hear that the White House is very much interested in this energy bill, but yet the Members on the other side voted against it.

MR. RHODES: It just shows that one can get a bill loused up so that even people who are for energy have to vote against it.

As I said, Tip O'Neill is a gregarious and engaging man. But he would rather go down in defeat time after time and veto after veto than ever to cooperate substantively with either the minority side or the Republican President of the United States.

THE MAJORITY WHIP: The job of the party Whip is essentially one of regulating the flow of communication between the leadership and the party rank-and-file. It is the Whip who informs the Members what the legislative schedule will be, once it has been determined by the Majority Leader. On key bills, it is up to the Whip to provide the party leadership with a projected vote count before the fact. He then works with the leadership to solidify existing support and convince the uncommitted Members.

While the job description of the Majority and Minority Whips are basically identical, their manner of selection is not. Republicans elect their Whip at the start of every Congress while, on the Democratic side, the Whip is chosen by the Speaker and the Majority Leader.

The current Majority Whip is Congressman John McFall of California. He is quiet, well-mannered, efficient and honorable. He gives the appearance of a distinguished small town banker and has a reputation for modesty and meticulousness.

His one character trait that sometimes impedes legislative

progress is an inherent distrust of all big business. One of the really genuine old school populists, McFall is almost impossible to communicate with when the interests of business are involved in a legislative dispute. This peculiar hangup is actually quite prevalent on the Democratic side. It has long amazed me how Democrats, who are "for" the creation of jobs, expansion of individual purchasing power and the like, can so oppose business. After all, it is a fact of economic life that business can produce infinitely more in the way of jobs than direct government spending. Major advances in such areas as space technology and energy development could not possibly have occurred in a climate where business did not have adequate capital for investment. The Democrats are all for the advances. But too often they try to deny the tools necessary to make these advances possible.

Throughout the congressional energy debate, for example, John McFall and other like-minded Democrats were adamant in their opposition to decontrolling domestic oil prices. The reason they used was that the large oil companies allegedly were ready to rip-off the American consumer. Our Republican counter to this charge was that Congress should go ahead and enact a "windfall profits" tax on the oil companies, thereby protecting the consumer against unfair-profit-taking at his expense. Ours was a completely logical answer. Yet Democrats would have nothing to do with it, so ingrained is their distrust of the business community.

THE CAUCUS CHAIRMAN: Of all the top leadership posts, the chairmanship of the Democratic Caucus is the most difficult to describe. The reason is that the Caucus does most of its work behind closed doors and out of the public view.

Following the lead of House Republicans, who opened up their Conference to the public and press in early 1975, the Democrats voted to partially open the Caucus. But it was only a halfway measure because whenever the Caucus meets to discuss House organization or particularly sensitive legislation, its rules provide that it meet in private. In other words, whenever the Caucus meets to flex its considerable muscle, it can do so far removed from public inspection.

Historically, the Democrats have used their Caucus to influence the organization of Congress and the fate of legislation to a far greater extent than have Republicans. In the early part of this century, the Democrats adopted rules that enabled the Caucus to bind individual Members to vote as the Caucus saw fit. As the years passed, instances of Caucus binding action became less and less frequent. The infrequency of usage [of Democratic binding action] coupled with the considerable pressure exerted by Republicans finally prompted a change in Caucus binding procedure in the 94th Congress. But it was only a cosmetic change because the Democratic Caucus still retains the power to bind Democrats on committees. The significance of this power was illustrated in February, 1975, when Democrats on the Rules committee were instructed by the Caucus to adopt a modified rule allowing separate floor votes on two amendments to the tax cut bill. The Caucus thus made it possible for the controversial amendment to repeal the oil and gas depletion allowance to be tacked onto the popular tax cut measure.

In contrast to the Democrats, the organization of Republican Members of the House, which we call the Conference, does not bind its Members' votes. Also in contrast to the other side, our Conference meetings are open to the public and the press.

The Democratic Caucus has lagged far behind the Republican Conference in other important aspects of democratic government. For example, it has clung tenaciously to the seniority system. There is something to be said for long experience as a factor in the selection of committee chairmen and ranking minority Members. It takes years to learn thoroughly the ins and outs of the legislative process, as well as to gain the confidence needed to maintain an adequate grip on headstrong and independent Members. But a strict seniority system, in which length of service is the only determinant of power and responsibility, is not conducive to quality leadership. For while length of service is an important factor, the individual who has served the longest is not necessarily the one best qualified to lead.

In recognition of the shortcomings of the seniority system, the House Republican Conference in 1970 appointed a special task force to study it and possibly recommend an alternative. Placed in charge of the task force was one of the most intelligent and capable Members of the House, Congressman Barber Conable of New York, who was to succeed me as chairman of the Republican Policy Committee when I was elected Minority Leader in 1973. After many long months of hard work, the Conable task force came up with a remarkable answer to the problems presented by the seniority system. It proposed that all ranking Republican Members on the committees be recommended at the start of each new Congress by the Republican Committee on Committees, but that these recommendations be either ratified or rejected by a mandatory secret ballot vote of the Republican Conference. Were it the prevailing view of a majority of House Republicans that a given ranking Member was not best qualified, he could easily be replaced with someone else.

After our progressive reform, the Democratic Caucus changed its method of selecting committee chairmen too. But once again the Caucus was only prepared to go so far. The Democrats provided that a vote by secret ballot on the fitness of a chairman could occur, providing that ten Democrats (it was later changed to four) are willing to stand for the purpose of demanding that such a vote take place. Obviously, those Members are not going to stand unless they are fairly certain that their view will prevail. For if the chairman in question survives the vote, he can make life miserable in a number of ways for those who dared challenge his authority.

As a result of the Caucus' policies, the archaic seniority system is still very much in existence. According to Ralph

Nader's *Congress Project,* "the seniority system is still 99% intact."

"Chairmen can throw their weight around because the seniority system insulates them from challenge," the Nader report added.

One of the more interesting developments in the 94th Congress has been the sudden rise in power of the current Caucus Chairman, Phillip Burton of California. A physically big man, Phil patrols the corridors of Capitol Hill with his face set in a perpetual scowl. His manner is brusque and aggressive and he may have more raw guts than any other Member. He wrested the chairmanship of the Caucus away from Congressman Bernie Sisk, another Californian, in a highly systematic way. He began his campaign well in advance of the '74 elections, buttonholing every sitting Democrat and promising to help raise campaign funds to many who pledged their support. As soon as the elections were over, he called on every new Democratic Member and insisted on firm commitments. When the Democratic Caucus met to organize, Burton was easily elected chairman.

Burton, a member of the liberal wing of a mainly liberal party, sees himself as a future Speaker of the House. Towards this end, he has formed an alliance with Wayne Hays, chairman of the House Administration Committee. Apparently, the alliance is also designed to help make Hays Majority Leader. Burton and Hays are similar in many respects. Both are tough, tireless and pay great attention to detail. They also share a thorough understanding of the nature of political power and know how to get what they want. It is entirely conceivable that the Burton-Hays alliance could someday prove successful on the basis of their sheer energy, hard work, and gall. Their success would occur at the expense of Tip O'Neill and other aspirants to the top rungs of the Democratic leadership.

———◆———

The Chairmen

WAYNE HAYS, HOUSE ADMINISTRATION COMMITTEE: Wayne
L. Hays is a paradox. In his capacity as Chairman of the House
Administration Committee,*Hays is arrogant, argumentative,
partisan and utterly ruthless. Few men in either chamber
understand political power as well as Wayne Hays. He knows
how to get it and once he has it, he knows what to do with it.
Chairman Hays is—and there is really no other way to put it—
a bully.

On the other hand, I can think of few Members who are
more valuable and adept in the treatment of sensitive foreign
policy matters. One of the top ranking Members on the House
International Relations Committee, Hays has a thorough feel
for the subtle interplay that goes on between foreign govern-
ments. He maintains a valuable network of contacts with foreign heads of state and dignitaries. During the sensitive negotiations that took place during the Turkish arms embargo,
Wayne Hays did as much as anyone to maintain some relationship with both Turkey and Greece. He handled himself in
this difficult crisis with skill and grace.

In his capacity as Chairman of the Committee on House
Administration, Hays is equally skilled but not so graceful.
Prior to his chairmanship, the House Administration Committee performed only routine bookkeeping chores. Wayne Hays'
genius transformed this obscure committee into a genuine
power base. In 1971, he succeeded in pushing through a bill
giving the House Administration Committee authority to issue
orders adjusting Members' office allowances and personal benefits without a ratifying vote by the full House. Since that time,
the Hays committee has issued at least 23 such orders. These
have resulted in a 116% increase in the number of trips a
Member can make to his District and back, an 85% increase
in a Member's stationery allowance, a 300% increase for
optional travel and a 75% increase in the funds available for
District office rentals. All of these goodies, and more, were

* On June 18, 1976, Mr. Hays announced that he would relinquish his chairmanship in response to the intense controversy surrounding his involvement in a
sex scandal. The author wrote this analysis at the height of Mr. Hays' power,
months before the scandals were made public.

received by grateful Members who did not have to cast an embarassing vote in order to get them.

Wayne Hays does for Members that which most of them want done but would never dare do for themselves. Therein lies the key to his immense power. With his congressional seat relatively safe, Hays willingly takes the heat for his colleagues. In return, he gets their support. A comment made by Hays on the Floor indicates that the Chairman is well aware of the service he performs:

> Mr. Speaker, it is pretty late but I would like to make the observation that the pay bill the other day passed this body by a vote of only 214 to 213, but I will be willing to take odds on it that those voting against it will be glad to take the pay increase.[3]

A testimony to Wayne Hays' strength is the fact that the 75 freshman Democrats who came to Washington determined to smash the seniority system, ousted three committee chairmen but left Hays alone. Many of the freshmen told the news media that they had been impressed by Hays' candor in a get acquainted meeting they had had with him. Maybe. A more realistic explanation is the fact that Hays, in his role as Chairman of the Democratic Congressional Committee, oversees the allocation of party funds to Democratic congressional candidates. The freshmen, most of whom would be facing stiff challenges in the next election, may have felt brave at the start of the 94th Congress . . . but not that brave.

RAY MADDEN, HOUSE RULES COMMITTEE: The responsibility of the Rules Committee is to regulate the flow of legislation from the various Committees to the House Floor in an orderly manner. The power of the Rules Committee is essentially twofold: First, since a bill usually requires a rule before it can reach the Floor, the Rules Committee can effectively kill a piece of legislation by denying it a rule. Second, because there are different kinds of rules—each one governing the types of changes that can be made on a bill when it reaches the Floor—

the Rules Committee can close off a wide range of legislative options if it so desires. A closed rule, for example, prohibits any Member from offering an amendment on the Floor. Former Congressman H. Allen Smith of California, who was the ranking Republican Member on Rules for a number of years, once stated: "The Rules Committee can propose anything that it wishes provided it is not unconstitutional. From that standpoint, it may be the most powerful committee in the House." [4]

The chairman of Rules is not elected by the Members of the majority party but is appointed by the Speaker. Prior to 1910, the Speaker served as chairman of Rules, a power which was stripped from that office in reaction to the excesses of Speaker Joe Cannon. From 1911 through 1974, the chairman of Rules was selected by the party machinery in the same way that other chairmen are chosen. In 1974, the majority changed the selection process again. This time the Speaker was given power to name his own Rules chairman.

Because he sits at the pleasure of the Speaker, the chairman of the Rules Committee invariably reflects the Speaker's brand of leadership. If the Speaker is strong, the Rules Committee chairman will likely be strong. If the Speaker is weak, so too will be the chairman of Rules. If the Speaker wants something done, the Rules committee chairman will move heaven and earth to do it. If the Speaker does not want something done, it is unusual for it to happen.

The current Rules Committee chairman is Ray J. Madden of Indiana. At 84, Madden is the oldest Member of Congress. A thoroughly decent and personally likeable man, Madden often gives the impression of not being completely tuned in or attentive, sometimes whistling throughout Rules Committee hearings and lecturing witnesses on subjects completely irrelevant to the business before the Committee. Other members of the Rules Committee have been known to walk out of hearings, completely frustrated by the periodic inability of the chairman to maintain a relevant train of thought.

As much as anyone else, Ray Madden is an entrenched member of the majority power structure.*

This chapter has been about power in Congress. It would be incomplete without mention of some of the forces which affect the legislative process from outside Congress. In many respects, the power from without can be even more formidable than the power from within.

For example, organized labor exerts considerable influence over the current Democratic Congress. George Meany, the indefatigable President of the AFL-CIO, is not an elected Member of Congress. Yet it seems frequently that Mr. Meany's power over legislation is as great as that of any committee chairman or member of the majority leadership. When Meany wants his way on Capitol Hill, it is rare that he does not get it.

Labor's influence over the Democratic Congress originates from the considerable amounts of money which it pumps into the campaign warchests of many Members. Besides money, big labor exerts considerable influence in congressional elections through in kind (non-monetary) contributions made by its Committee on Political Education (COPE). Equipped with computerized lists of union members, the oftentimes massive army of labor volunteers can have a palpable impact on the outcome of a congressional contest. Labor's impact is particularly significant in special elections, where it can concentrate its forces to maximum advantage.

Many Democratic Members come to rely on big labor's money and political clout to such an extent that they find it very difficult, if not impossible, to vote against the wishes of labor. George Meany has openly boasted that the Members he sent to the 94th Congress voted his way 95% of the time.

It is interesting to see big labor at work on Capitol Hill. There is one red-haired, ubiquitous woman lobbyist for the AFL-CIO whom I call "Madame Defarge." Like the character in *A Tale of Two Cities* who sat by the guillotine knitting

* On May 4, 1976, Mr. Madden was defeated in the Indiana primary in his bid for an 18th term.

furiously at the climactic moments, "Madame Defarge" stands by the doors to the House floor during a vote in which labor has an interest. Her presence is always a signal to me that George Meany intends to get his way. As Democratic Members file by, she gestures thumbs up or thumbs down, thereby instructing them how to vote.

Another significant outside influence is the so-called Education Lobby. Comprised of the National Education Association and the American Federation of Teachers, it has become one of the most powerful of the pressure groups. The Education Lobby has some access to money, but more important than money is its peerless ability to communicate. A Member who earns the antipathy of the Education Lobby can count on receiving a barrage of angry letters from school teachers and parents in his district.

Evidence of the Education Lobby's power is best found in the number of times Congress has granted full funding for federal aid to elementary and secondary education programs. A figure is set forth in the authorizing legislation, a ballpark guess as to the maximum amount which could be spent. The figure is intended to represent a ceiling, not a floor. Instead, various pressure groups, chief among them the Education Lobby, have banded together to demand full funding, as if the ceiling were actually a floor. More times than not, the efforts of the Education Lobby to obtain full funding have proved successful.

There are other outside influences which have a major impact on the outcome of legislation in Congress. Just about all of them have one thing in common: a desire to preserve the current Democratic majority. True, there are some groups which gravitate more towards Republicans, such as business associations with a stake in the free enterprise system. But their impact, compared to that of organized labor and the others, is minimal, for the simple reason that Republicans are essentially without any congressional power. The power is now with the Democrats. Most pressure groups understand this and work hard to cultivate appropriate alliances.

Even if a chairman or member of the majority leadership occasionally goes against the wishes of a particular pressure group, it is unlikely that the group would want to do anything that might result in his being replaced. "We <u>know</u> what kind of an S.O.B. this one is," they say. "We might get a <u>worse</u> S.O.B. if we don't keep him."

What I am describing is an atmosphere in which all sources of power—from inside and outside Congress—are working hard to preserve the status quo. Were the power scales tipped and Republicans placed in charge of Congress, the pressure groups would be starting completely from scratch. They would be less likely to get their way because their considerable storehouse of political I.O.U.'s would be depleted.

If ever there is to be change in Congress, it will have to come from the people themselves.

4   The Underachievers

"The weaker the leadership and the more external the demands, the slower will be the lawmaking."
—Richard F. Fenno, Jr. *Professor of Political Science, University of Rochester*

CONGRESS doesn't work as it should. It responds to challenge and initiative slowly, if at all. Out of touch with the people of America, this present Congress is a pitiful helpless giant, devoid of coordination or purpose.

The Democratic Congress was evaluated by the *Washington Post's* Mary Russell in the language of the unforgettable Watergate tapes: ". . . its position on reform was (inaudible), its action in the public interest (unintelligible) and its performance as a whole an (expletive deleted)."

The view of Walter Taylor, Capitol Hill reporter for the *Washington Star,* was also negative and direct. "The Democrats" who control Congress, wrote Taylor, "are squabbling and second-guessing among themselves . . . seemingly ripped apart over ways of dealing with some of the most pressing economic problems."

The American people concurred. In early 1974, Louis Harris reported that the public's rating of the job performance of the Congress had plummeted to an all-time low of 21%. In another poll Harris reported that public confidence in Congress has dropped as low as 13%.

One of the big reasons for the intensity of the criticism directed against Congress is the fact that the Democrats have such an overwhelming number of Members. If they cannot produce results with one of the largest majorities in modern history, the American people feel they will never be able to produce.

In this sense, the sweeping gains made by the Democrats in the 1974 election could very well turn out to be the unluckiest thing to have happened to them since the decision of Dwight David Eisenhower to run as a Republican. The two-to-one edge in favor of the Democrats has served to dramatize the weaknesses of Democratic leaders. Their warts have been exposed as never before. It must pain them severely.

Republicans would like to forget the 1974 elections. For the party, the election results were a tragic end to a year-long nightmare. Watergate rode as a monkey on the back of just about every Republican congressional candidate. Although I did so at just about every opportunity, it did little good to explain that congressional Republicans had had nothing to do with Watergate. The American people had been outraged by the scandal and felt the need to strike back at someone. Since Richard Nixon was no longer around, the only available targets were Republican congressional candidates. By holding congressional Republicans accountable for Watergate, many voters were guilty of a gross double standard. I do not recall that the voters reacted with any great degree of anger in the past to either the Bobby Baker scandal or the Billy Sol Estes affair, two skeletons in the Democrats' closet.

Nevertheless, many people seemed determined to punish blameless congressional Republicans because of the abuses committed by Nixon.

The Nixon pardon only served to aggravate the problems faced by Republican candidates in the fall of 1974. Still, in my opinion President Ford's decision to pardon his predecessor was a necessary one. Given the high degree of publicity, it is doubtful that the former President could have received a fair trial (an opinion shared by former Special Prosecutor Archibald Cox, a respected lawyer and a Democrat). There was also the question of his physical and mental health. There were many who felt that he had paid the ultimate penalty for his mistakes and had suffered enough. More important, the country had suffered enough. The prospects of a sensational trial extending for a year or more was one that nobody save the die-hard Nixon-haters relished. President Ford concluded that the best way to put Watergate in the past was to grant a pardon to his predecessor.

The reasons for the pardon were sound but the timing could not have been worse. Instead of preparing the public for the controversial pardon that was to come, the President announced his decision with very little warning. I first learned of the President's decision when I arrived home after a Sunday morning round of golf and found three network film crews camped on my front lawn. (Later I learned that the President had tried to telephone me earlier that day.)

The American people do not take kindly to surprises from their Government, particularly surprises of such magnitude. The Nixon pardon, well-conceived but horribly timed and poorly explained, stirred up the emotions of the public once again—to the clear disadvantage of Republican candidates for Congress. The pardon significantly contributed to the substantial increase in Democratic strength in the 94th Congress.

After the '74 elections, the Democrats outnumbered us in the House by a margin of 291 to 144. In the Senate there were 61 Democrats and only 38 Republicans. Their two-to-one advantage gave them a numerical veto-proof House since it requires a two-thirds vote to override a presidential veto. It would have been veto-proof in reality but for the ability of the minority side to maintain a high degree of cohesion on most attempted veto overrides.

The huge size of the Democratic majority made it incumbent upon the Democratic leadership to produce legislative results. Said Democratic National Committee Chairman Robert Strauss: "There has never been a time when the Members (of Congress) have been more sensitive to the fact that the people want some action. If we don't perform, we'll be held accountable . . . and we should be!"

Democratic congressional leaders, seeing the handwriting on the wall, did their very best to rally their troops into action. Speaker Albert talked proudly about the "mandate" the voters of the country had given his party. Congressman John Brademas of Indiana, also a member of the majority leadership, promised the people "congressional government." Most everyone expected that the 94th Congress, controlled by one of the largest majorities in modern history, would be able to enact a legislative program of its own.

But things didn't turn out that way. Instead, the troubled 94th embarked on a course of blunder and intrigue.

The Turkish Aid Fiasco

Congress had every right to be appalled by the Turkish military invasion of the island of Cyprus in July, 1974. This use of armed aggression could not be countenanced.

The Turkish action, however, was not quite as one-sided as many pro-Greek spokesmen maintained. After all, a Greek faction had been directly responsible for the July 15 coup which resulted in the forced overthrow of Cypriot President Archbishop Makarios. It had also been responsible for the subsequent installation of a regime headed by Nikos Sampson, a man who possessed a long record of violence against the sizable Turkish minority on Cyprus. When Turkey decided to invade Cyprus, it did so at the behest of these Turkish Cypriots, many of whom feared for their lives. Turkey cited as justification for her military action Article 3 of the 1959 Treaty of Zurich, which specifically gives her the right to take action to preserve the status quo on Cyprus. So it was a complex issue, and neither side had any exclusive claim to virtue.

The Ford Administration was working hard behind the scenes to bring Turkey and Greece to the negotiating table. Given Secretary of State Henry Kissinger's impressive track record in the Middle East, there was reasonable hope for successful negotiation. Until Congress got into the act, that is.

Spurred on by a vocal Greek American lobby and led by three Democratic Members of the House of Greek descent— John Brademas of Indiana, Paul Sarbanes of Maryland and Peter Kyros of Maine—and one who was not of Greek descent, Benjamin Rosenthal of New York (although of Jewish descent, we came to refer to him as 'The Super Greek') Congress imposed an embargo on all U.S. foreign aid to Turkey until "substantial progress" had been made towards settlement of the Cyprus dispute. This action was ill-conceived for it implicitly placed the entire blame for the crisis on the Turks, one of our most loyal allies.

It took nearly a full year for the Cyprus issue to come to a head. During that time, Congress softened its original strident position and agreed to postpone the embargo while the Administration worked on a negotiated settlement. Congress suspended the embargo twice—once in October, 1974, and again in December. On February 5, 1975, the embargo went into effect.

The reaction of the Turks, a very proud people, was entirely predictable. They felt that they had been treated unjustly. Because the source of this "injustice" was the United States, which Turkey had long regarded as a strong ally, their resentment was all the more acute. Inevitably, Turkey searched for a way to strike back. She did not have to search far.

Turkey plays a key role in United States defense and foreign policy. The U.S. maintains 26 military bases and four intelligence outposts in Turkey. They are our intelligence ear to the Soviet Union and because of Turkey's geographical position, are literally irreplaceable.

Turkey's role in N.A.T.O. is also critical. She controls the only route connecting the Black Sea and the Mediterranean. Were Turkey to withdraw from N.A.T.O., its southern flank would be exposed and thus the entire Mediterranean community, including Greece ironically, would be endangered.

Therefore the Cyprus crisis was more than a local dispute between Turkey and Greece. It was a crisis involving American national security, the future of N.A.T.O., and the stability of the whole eastern Mediterranean.

The Senate, more experienced than the House in foreign policy, recognized the serious implications of the embargo policy and on May 19, 1975, voted to end it. This action was unacceptable to the House where the Greek lobby had a far more profound influence. Another bill emerged. It would permit the shipment of military arms already purchased from the Unted States by Turkey. It would also allow Turkey to purchase additional arms on the commercial market in the U.S.A. In other words, we would give the Turks what rightfully belonged to them. It would be a small gesture, but one which would ease the rising tension.

The bill came to the House Floor on July 24 and was defeated by a vote of 223-206. The very next day, Turkey did what proponents of the embargo said it would never do. It ordered the United States to suspend its operations in Turkey at once and prepare to vacate its bases. The problem had now become a foreign policy crisis of the highest order.

During the week of July 28, an all-out effort was made to revive the bill. Since Congress was set to adjourn for a month-long recess on July 31, supporters of the effort had to race against time. We went right down to the wire, staying in session late into the evening of the 31st, long after all other pending business had been completed. While Members of the House waited on pins and needles for the Senate to act on the bill so that it could be brought to the Floor for a vote, the pro-Greek forces tried repeatedly to force an adjournment. Six times a motion was made to adjourn. Six times the motion failed.

Finally, around 11 p.m., the Senate acted affirmatively and rushed the bill by special messenger over to the House. Only one last obstacle stood in the way of a House vote: the absence of a rule under which the bill could be debated. Despite the chairman's opposition and the lateness of the hour, it was assumed that the Rules Committee would meet in its room just above the House Floor and grant a rule in a matter of minutes.

It was well-known that Ray Madden, the 84-year old Chairman of the House Rules committee, was opposed to the bill and favored a continuation of the arms embargo. Earlier that evening, while the House waited for the Senate to act, he had explained that his opposition was born at several picnics he had recently attended in his district:

> For the Information of the Members I have made three trips back home in the last month. During the recess over the Fourth of July, I was back there and the last two Sundays I attended several picnics of my constituents.
>
> Mr. Speaker, these picnic gatherings were almost unanimous in criticism of this Turkish grant legislation. I did not hear a person there speak for it, and there were speeches made and I received comments for fighting it and voting against it.
>
> Now 2 weeks ago Sunday, and the newspapers are out there if Members want to check on it, I attended a Greek picnic . . . the response against this Turkey grant was almost unanimous.[5]

Just as I heard the messenger's ceremonious announcement, "Mr. Speaker, a message from the Senate," a Republican Congressman hurried up to me at the minority leadership table.

"You're not going to believe this, John," he said breathlessly, "but I just saw Ray Madden climb into his car and take off.

It looked to me like he was leaving for the night!"

I rose quickly and grabbed the microphone. Once recognized, I informed the Members that Chairman Madden had apparently left Capitol Hill to go home.

Within moments, the House Floor had erupted into pandemonium. Members were running up and down the aisles like extras in a Keystone Cops comedy. No one seemed to know what to make of the situation. At the Republican leadership table we huddled in a last-ditch effort to find a way for Congress to work its will before time ran out. It was decided that John Anderson, an able and articulate member of the Republican leadership as well as a member of the Rules Committee, would make a parliamentary inquiry aimed at establishing the fact that in Madden's absence the Speaker could appoint a temporary Chairman of Rules.

Speaker Albert ruled against John Anderson on the grounds that the Turkish arms embargo was not a critical enough matter to justify his appointing a temporary chairman. I rose to ask the Speaker to reconsider his ruling. "I cannot believe that the Chair is ruling that it is not possible for the House to instruct the chairman of a committee to call a meeting of that committee and, his having failed to do so, to instruct somebody else to call a meeting."

The Speaker was not swayed. "The Chair will not listen to any further argument on the issue on which the Chair has ruled," he shouted. "This could go on all night . . ."

With all legislative avenues sealed off, Congress thus adjourned for a vacation without acting.

The entire Turkish embargo issue illustrates perfectly why the founding fathers placed most of the day-to-day responsibility for foreign policy in the hands of the Executive. Because Congress controls the purse and has sole authority to declare war, it plays a key foreign policy role. But there is no way that 535 individuals can take the place of the Secretary of State. Congress is too large and complex to fashion short-term foreign policy. As was demonstrated by

HELLO, MR. PRESIDENT?...THIS IS THE SPEAKER OF THE HOUSE CALLING. LISTEN, JERRY, THANKS FOR CONSULTING US ON THIS RUSSIAN INVASION THING. SORRY I COULDN'T GET BACK TO YOU SOONER, BUT YOUR PROPOSAL FOR A COUNTERATTACK WAS TABLED IN COMMITTEE....BUT WE HAVE COME UP WITH A COMPROMISE MEASURE— A RIDER TO THE CONSUMER PROTECTION BILL....NOW, WE'RE HOPEFUL WE CAN HAVE IT ON YOUR DESK BEFORE OUR GROUND HOG DAY RECESS.......

the Turkish embargo controversy, Congress tends to react emotionally and politically, and therefore can make a bad situation worse.

The Energy Crisis

It is ironic that the energy issue—a problem every bit as serious as Vietnam and Watergate—is a relatively simple problem to solve. The Arab Nations arbitrarily embargoed the shipment of oil to the United States during the fall of 1973. They then hiked world oil prices by more than 400%. Hit without warning, America needed to make some hard energy decisions . . . and fast.

Congress began struggling to enact an emergency energy law during the height of the fuel crisis in December, 1973. We stayed in session until Christmas Eve that year, only to adjourn without taking action. The next two years were a nightmare of indecision, delay and arrogance. Federal Energy Administrator Frank Zarb and his aides almost took up residence on Capitol Hill while they testified before the spate of committees claiming energy jurisdiction and tried their repeated best to cajole key Democratic Members of Congress reluctant to cooperate with the other side. We seemed light years away from the 1950's, when even the toughest Democratic leaders willingly cooperated with Republicans on matters of national importance.

Aside from moving forward with the development of alternate energy sources, the obvious solution to the crisis was to find a way to increase the domestic production of oil. This could best be accomplished by decontrolling old domestic oil prices, which had been frozen at $5.25 a barrel since 1971. Since that time production costs had risen appreciably, so that it had become unprofitable for oil companies to move ahead with exploration and drilling. By permitting old oil to reflect its true market value, we would provide the oil companies with an incentive to develop the substantial known oil reserves located within the United States.

The President developed a specific decontrol plan which would ensure that the decontrol process be gradual and the economy not unduly jolted. His plan also provided for a windfall profits tax on the oil companies to prevent the American consumer from being ripped off. The President's plan was strongly supported by almost every member of the Republican minority. Also, public opinion polls taken throughout 1975 showed that a sizable majority of Americans favored decontrol of oil prices. It was, from the very beginning, the only logical route to follow.

The Democratic leadership did not agree. They were hung up on the question of short-term fuel prices. Petrified at the thought of having to face the electorate after having supported higher gasoline prices, they refused even to consider the President's reasonable decontrol plan. Every time any of us on the minority side would make the case for decontrol, one of them would say that decontrol was out of the question because it would cause prices to go up. The American people do not deserve higher fuel prices, they would insist.

Of course the American people do not deserve higher fuel prices. But neither did they deserve the long lines at the gasoline pumps that resulted from insufficient supplies. Rarely in my memory has the division between the two congressional parties been so wide as it has been over energy . . . nor so frustrating.

Appalled by the Democrats' stubborn opposition to decontrol, Lindley H. Clark, Jr. wrote in the *Wall Street Journal*: "If there isn't an energy crisis now, Congress is showing us that it knows how to create one." [6]

In his 1975 State of the Union Message at the start of the First Session of the 94th Congress, President Ford resubmitted his plan for gradual decontrol of domestic oil. Soon after, the Democratic leadership outlined a different energy plan. Its key feature was an extensive increase in the gasoline tax aimed at encouraging energy conservation. This plan was soon rejected by numerous Members of the majority. A power struggle within Democratic ranks ensued to determine who was "king of the mountain" on energy. Congressman Al Ullman of Oregon, who replaced Wilbur Mills as chairman of the important House Committee on Ways and Means, went to work on a program of his own. The Ullman plan was similarly shot down, mainly because the high ranking members of the majority were reluctant to stand aside and allow the new chairman to take center stage.

The frustration caused by Congress' inability to act on energy was ably articulated by Irving Kristol in the *Wall Street Journal:* "One could understand that Congress might find it painful to make a choice between alternatives," wrote Mr. Kristol. "One could understand if it faltered, moved reluctantly, displayed signs of confusion. What is not comprehensible is the apparent determination of Congress to refuse to act at all—indeed, to deny the necessity of choice. Instead, Congress is desperately looking for scapegoats in the oil industry or the Executive Branch or wherever." [7]

John Gardner, Chairman of Common Cause, the non-partisan citizen's lobby, was also outraged. Referring to the "congressional paralysis" on energy, Gardner asked: "After Watergate, the Congress talked bravely of taking leadership. Where is that leadership now?"

By the summer of 1975, even leading Democrats had had enough. Senate Majority Leader Mike Mansfield, never one to mince words, blasted the failure of his own party to come up with an energy program. He blamed the proliferation of committees, each one studying energy and each one jockeying for power, as the chief problem. "The way things are going, we haven't got a leg to stand on," Senator Mansfield declared. "We can't put the blame on the President. He has gone more than halfway."

In time, the logic of decontrol began to penetrate the minds

of the Democrats. Because of partisan maneuvering, however, still more time was wasted. A new logjam resulted when
Interstate and Foreign Commerce Committee Chairman Har-
ley Staggers and Chairman John Dingell of the subcommittee
on Energy and Power insisted that decontrol be accomplished
not by a quick Executive decontrol plan but through legislation drafted slowly by Congress.

As one Democratic freshman confessed to me during this
insane waiting period, "We can't support anything the President proposes because Congress should have its own plan.
The fact that he's a Republican President just makes it easier
for us to get away with opposing him."

Finally, in December of 1975—30 months after Congress
first started grappling with the energy crisis—an "emergency"
energy program was passed. Decontrol would be permitted,
but not until after the 1976 elections. The stipulation con-
stitutes positive proof that the main concern of the Democratic
majority was the prospect of having to face the voters in an
election year after having allowed fuel prices to go up.

A succinct analysis of Congress' conduct during the prolonged energy debate appeared in the *Baltimore Sun*. "The
nation's energy problem," the *Sun* concluded, "was dealt with
not on its merits but on the basis of its politics." [8] That is a
sad commentary on the calibre of Democratic congressional
leadership today. Equally sad was the year-end "congressional
report card" of *Time* Magazine. *Time* gave the 94th Congress good marks in some areas; but on energy legislation, the
grades were "D" for effort and "F" in performance.

The Pay Raise Rip-Off

Members of Congress have always approached legislation
concerning their own salaries with great trepidation. On the
one hand, they feel that they are underpaid in relation to
what they could be making in the private sector. On the other
hand, they are acutely sensitive to the political hazards in-

volved in raising their own pay during times of high inflation and unemployment.

In 1967, Congress discovered a clever way out of this dilemma: it established a new commission to recommend pay rates for Members of Congress and top executive and judicial branch officials. By law, the Commission's recommendations were given to the President and incorporated into his annual budget. The law provided that Congress had 30 legislative days in which to pass a "motion of disapproval." If such a motion was not approved, the raises went into effect automatically. The Democrats adroitly provided that the required "motion of disapproval" not be a privileged motion— meaning that no individual Member could get it out of committee and bring it to the Floor without the acquiescence of the majority leadership.

This virtually ensured approval of all pay raises. It also spared Members the embarrassment of having to vote themselves a pay increase. They could tell the people in their district that they were dead set against the raise but were powerless to change "the system."

The 94th Congress further subverted the system when it passed a bill to give Members of Congress and other top government officials an annual pay raise tied automatically to the cost of living. As the cost of living goes up, so too does a Member's pay. He will never have to cast a vote on the matter!

I was first told of this proposal early in 1975. Phil Burton, the Democratic Caucus Chairman, approached me one afternoon on the House Floor to explain the plan. I could scarcely believe what I was hearing. I had never in my life voted against a merited congressional pay raise and had never felt that it had hurt me back home. But the thought of Members of Congress profiting from increases in the cost-of-living— realizing that Congress has more to do with the cost-of-living than anyone else—struck me as utterly repugnant. I told Burton then that I would never go along on this issue.

From that day on, I was purposely cut out of all strategy sessions and talks related to the pay raise plan. The backers of the proposal were fully aware of its controversial nature and were counting on having the element of surprise on their side. As *Congressional Quarterly* correctly observed:

> They (backers of the bill) worked on the assumption that routine handling would doom it to failure by the time the measure had worked its way through both House and Senate Committees and gone to each chamber for a vote. Planners feared that the debate and the public reaction would have generated too much opposition.[9]

The powers behind the pay raise proposal—among them Speaker Albert, Majority Leader O'Neill, and Burton in the House and Gale McGee in the Senate—selected as the target date for their bill the week of July 28 when Congress was scheduled to adjourn for a month-long recess. They figured that the hectic atmosphere that precedes a congressional recess would work to their advantage.

Their legislative vehicle was H.R. 2559, a relatively minor bill authorizing a job safety program for postal workers. This vehicle was chosen with great care, since it would have to come before the Senate Post Office and Civil Service Committee, of which Gale McGee is Chairman. H.R. 2559 passed the House on June 16, was sent to the Senate, and was routinely deposited in Senator McGee's committee. On July 25 it emerged from his committee with the controversial pay raise formula tacked on. Four days later it cleared the Senate.

There is simply no way to describe the blinding speed at which the pay raise bill hit the House. Less than 24 hours after the Senate vote, the House Rules Committee agreed to suspend normal procedures and allow the House to vote that same day.

The bill was brought up without fanfare, and took its opponents completely by surprise. It was one of those rare times when the effort to defeat a bill could not begin in earnest until the voting had started. Opponents of the bill stationed themselves squarely in front of all the entrances to the Floor and as Members came in, they pleaded with them to vote No.

The voting remained close from beginning to end. Each time it appeared as though one side were pulling away, shouts of encouragement and cheers of joy could be heard above the din on the House Floor. That seemed to act as an incentive to the other side to pull even, and it did.

When the time had expired, it appeared as though the measure had been defeated by a narrow margin. But Speaker Albert refused to gavel the vote closed. Ignoring the angry cries of Members opposed to the bill, the Speaker asked repeatedly, "Are there any Members who desire to change their votes?"

By now the situation on the Floor was chaotic. From the majority side, several Members were hustled down the crowded runway to the well. In barely audible voices, they changed their votes. Speaker Albert gaveled the vote closed and announced that the pay raise had passed by a single vote.

It took the Democratic Congress thirty months to enact an emergency energy bill; yet a bill to provide for automatic pay raises for Members of Congress was whisked through the legislative process with lightning speed. Now it is a new part of the system, a system that will not be changed until the majority leadership is changed.

The Way It Used To Be

There is no doubt in my mind that I have been privileged to serve in Congress during the careers of two of the most able congressional leaders in the history of the Republic. It makes little difference that they were Democrats and I am a Republican . . . Sam Rayburn and Lyndon Johnson knew how to make Congress work.

Both men were fiercely loyal to their party. They were incredibly strong leaders who made skillful use of the powers

① ENERGY BILL ② GUN CONTROL ③ CONGRESSIONAL CAMPAIGN REFORM ④ TAX REFORM

⑤ WYMAN–DURKIN QUESTION ⑥ CIA ABUSES ⑦ FORD VETOES ⑧ CONGRESSIONAL PAY RAISE

available to the majority leadership. They hated to lose and they rarely did.

Speaker Rayburn ("Mr. Sam" as he was affectionately called by his colleagues) is best remembered for having laid down his famous dictum to new Members of Congress: "In order to get along, you have to go along." He is also remembered for his "Board of Education." The 'Board' was one of the Speaker's hideaway offices to which he would invite from time to time various Members to discuss the business of Congress over bourbon and other spirits. Speaker Rayburn listened to what all had to say, and then instructed his 'Board meetings' the way it was to be the following day. Only rarely did subsequent events deviate substantially from the Speaker's plans.

Rayburn, incidentally, occupied room H-231 in the Capitol, the office I now occupy. Many have been the times that I wish walls could talk!

The stories about the techniques used by Lyndon Johnson to get his way in the Senate are similar. I doubt that Johnson ever went to the Floor for an important vote without having a very good idea beforehand what the outcome would be.

There were exceptions, of course, but Johnson could be counted on to rise to the occasion. One time, for example, the Majority Leader miscalculated his vote total by one, the margin he needed to win passage of a particular bill. As the roll call was about to end, Johnson whirled around on the Floor, pointed to a Member of the majority who had voted the "wrong" way, and shouted across the room: "Change your vote!" The Senator looked stunned, not knowing quite what to do.

"Change your vote!" Johnson demanded again. The vote was changed and the bill passed.

In the 1950's, the situation in Government resembled that of today in that both the House and Senate were controlled by Democratic majorities, and the President was a Republican. However, today the division of party control has resulted in stalemate between the legislative and executive branches, whereas in the 1950's there was none. Sam Rayburn and Lyndon Johnson deserve a great deal of the credit for this. They were both eager to score partisan victories and did so often. But there was another factor that figured heavily in their thinking priorities: the national interest.

"I am not afraid as long as I do what seems right," Speaker Rayburn once said.

On the other side of the Capitol, Senate Majority Leader Johnson said he had "one yardstick that I try to measure things by. Is this in the national interest? Is this what I believe is best for my country?"

Let there be no doubt that both men were great Democrats who wanted the very best for their party. They could be as partisan as anyone. But they also wanted the best for the country. The two desires are not always compatible.

Rayburn and Johnson recognized a duty, as leaders of the majority in Congress, to produce legislative results for the country. This often meant willingly cooperating with the Republican President—despite their partisanship, despite their individual strength, despite all other things. Ralph K. Huitt, a political scientist who worked for Lyndon Johnson in the Senate, analyzed his former boss' relationship with the Republican Executive:

> Lyndon Johnson, as majority leader, did not work with a Democratic President, and it would be presumptuous to speculate about hypothetical relationships. But he *did* work with a Republican President for six years, and this relationship is illuminating. Johnson regarded the Presidency as the one office in the American system which can give national leadership. He scoffed at the notion that his own initiative, in the absence of presidential leadership of Congress, made him a kind of 'prime minister.' His own description of his activity was that 'we prod him (Eisenhower) into doing everything we can get him to do, and when he does something good we give him a 21-gun salute.' He consistently refused to turn the Democrats in the Senate loose to attack Eisenhower at will, believing that no President can be cut down

without hurting the presidency itself—with the American people the losers. Johnson worked with Eisenhower with dispassionate professionalism, supporting or differing with him as he believed he should.[10]

In 1958, a year during which the country plunged to a severe recession, Congress enacted a housing bill that resulted in the creation of half a million new jobs. Rayburn and Johnson made sure that the bill which finally emerged was one that President Eisenhower would agree to sign into law. In order to accomplish this, they consulted with the Administration. They also made several concessions. Rayburn and Johnson were sharply criticized by Members of their own party for cooperating with the Republicans. But as a result, the country got a badly-needed housing program.

In the House, Speaker Rayburn, answering his Democratic critics, said, "It doesn't matter to me what Party gets the credit."

On the Senate side, Majority Leader Johnson confronted his critics with a question: "What do you want?" he demanded, "houses or a housing issue?"

The willingness of Democratic leaders Rayburn and Johnson to cooperate with the Republican President in the national interest was particularly evident in foreign policy. There used to be an old saying around Congress that "Politics stops at the water's edge," meaning that when it came to foreign policy, Members were neither Democrats nor Republicans but Americans. That philosophy is no longer prevalent (to wit: the Turkish embargo and the attempts to hold Secretary of State Kissinger in contempt of Congress).

I cannot recall a single instance in which either Rayburn or Johnson was in the least way partisan in a foreign policy matter. In fact, my recollection is that they went to extraordinary lengths to prevent partisanship.

Some of the bloodiest Conferences between the House and Senate I have ever attended concerned foreign aid appropriations bills. The Foreign Operations Subcommittee of the

House Appropriations Committee, chaired by Congressman Otto Passman of Louisiana, constantly tried to cut foreign aid to the bone. The Senate counterpart, on the other hand, always favored increasing aid at least to the level suggested by the President.

Senate Majority Leader Lyndon Johnson was frequently a conferee on these bills, as was I. In the midst of heated negotiations, Lyndon Johnson would often lift his large frame up from his chair and duck out into the hall to confer with officials of the Eisenhower Administration. He would ask them whether or not they could "live with" various compromises worked out in Conference. Then he would return to the room, urge approval of whatever had been worked out, and move ahead to the next point of contention. It was a very impressive performance.

In the Democratic Congresses of the 1950's, there was no doubt who ran things. Sam Rayburn and Lyndon Johnson did. They were strong-willed and tough, ambitious and aggressive men who were constantly looking for new ways to improve their party's fortunes. They were capable of launching some of the most partisan attacks ever known to man.

But, as I have pointed out, there was something else— another dimension—that transcended partisan politics in those days. Call it the national interest. Call it leadership. Call it what you will. When it came to the real business of running the country—of choosing between legislative results or stalemate—they chose cooperation over confrontation virtually every time.

They worked with a Republican President. They also worked with the Republican minority. Speaker Rayburn explained his relationship with House Minority Leader Charles Halleck in these words: "We have to work together in the House if we are going to get anything accomplished. So we have an agreement as to how we are going to do it."

Democratic Party leadership of today is but a shadow of its former self. Members on the majority side—particularly the committee chairmen—are permitted to do their own thing regardless of the effect that such freedom may have on the legislative process.

The current leadership does not cooperate with either the Executive or the minority. The watchword in this Congress seems to be opposition for the sake of creating issues for use in the next election. The majority leadership does not appear to care about producing legislative results now. The leadership permits bills to pass which it knows will be vetoed, when prior consultation and some compromise with the Executive and the minority would make many vetoes unnecessary.

Even in foreign policy there is very little willingness on the part of the majority leadership to cooperate with the President. Partisan politics used to end at the water's edge.

In fairness to the present Democratic leaders, I should mention at least two disadvantages they face that their predecessors did not.

First, the congressional process itself is not what it used to be. The institutional deterioration, particularly within the committee structure, is not to be believed. Rayburn and Johnson presided over Democratic Congresses, but those Democratic Congresses were not as entrenched as they are now. In those days, the committees were more responsive to the leadership, because the committee jurisdictions were more clearly defined. Today's majority leadership is forced to work with a committee structure that is hopelessly confused. It seemingly cannot be reformed from within the ranks of the present Democratic majority.

A second disadvantage faced by the current majority leadership is the very size of the majority. The current majority is too big for its own good. The membership is like a herd of raging buffalo that the leadership is powerless to control. The object of each party in any congressional election is to have as many of its own candidates win as possible. But there is a point beyond which the numbers actually work to the disadvantage of the majority, a point of diminishing returns. This fact was well-understood by Sam Rayburn. The former Speaker, a staunch Democrat, warned before his death of the danger presented by a majority that is too large.

The American people should understand the brutal fact that a Congress overloaded with Democrats cannot act even when a majority of its Members want to. This was the conclusion reached by the *Washington Post*, after it conducted an extensive survey of House Members during the summer of 1975. "The most striking material from the survey," the *Post* reported, "is the evidence that this legislative body often cannot effectively express its own majority sentiments, let alone the desires of the American people." The issue of forced busing was cited as an example "where the House is in step with public opinion." A majority of the American people oppose forced busing; a majority of their representatives do too. Yet the House has been unable even to hold hearings on anti-busing legislation. Why? Because the chairman of the House Judiciary Committee has refused to do so.

"It is," the *Post* concluded, "an issue that undoubtedly contributes to the public notion that the system doesn't work."

The system doesn't work because the system is old and in desperate need of repair and because the current majority— the party that runs Congress—is incapable of making these repairs. They have tried . . . and they have failed.

5   The Agony of Reform

"Progress is a nice word. But change is its motivator. And change has its enemies."

—Robert F. Kennedy

RICHARD BOLLING is a Democrat who has represented Missouri's Fifth congressional district since 1949. He is brilliant *(New Times* Magazine chose him as one of the "ten brightest" Congressmen). A protege of former Speaker Rayburn and a close friend of current Speaker Albert, he is hard-working, ambitious, and easily one of the most knowledgeable Members of Congress.

Bolling is the third ranking Democrat on the powerful Rules Committee and the author of two excellent books on the House of Representatives. He knows as well as anyone why the system won't work and has worked harder than most to make the changes that must be made.

On January 31, 1973 the House gave Dick Bolling an

important chance to bring his knowledge of congressional procedure to bear when it created a Select Committee on Committees. The Select Committee, which had the enthusiastic bipartisan support of Speaker Albert and then Minority Leader Gerald R. Ford, was given a mandate to remodel the tired and confused network of House Committees. Not since 1946 had the committee system been significantly changed. Reform was long overdue.

Bolling was named chairman of the Select Committee, with Congressman Dave Martin of Nebraska serving as the ranking Republican Member.

The history of the Bolling reform plan is a tortured one. The product of 14 months of exhaustive hearings that cost the taxpayers $1.5 million, the plan hit the cloakrooms late in 1973 with hurricane-like force. Few had expected the Committee to propose the extensive overhaul that it did. Some of us were pleasantly surprised. Others were not so pleased.

The Bolling plan was received by Members of the House in much the same way that the draft lottery used to be received on college campuses: each Member frantically searched to determine how he would be affected by the proposed reforms. Not surprisingly, those Members whose power and prestige stood a chance of being diminished by the changes were up in arms. Since the majority controls the power in Congress, the grumblings on the Democratic side were pretty loud.

The Democratic Caucus jumped into the act. By secret ballot, the majority elected to send the Bolling plan to a Caucus subcommittee with instructions to put together an alternate, less dramatic set of reforms.

Early in October, 1974, both plans were brought to the House Floor for a week-long debate. Most Republicans rallied behind the Bolling version, but were far outnumbered. The watered-down substitute was enacted instead.

Later, I invited Dick Bolling to appear with me on a 30-minute television program to discuss the subject of congressional reform. The program, which I tape monthly for an

Arizona television station, features a prominent guest, at least two reporters and myself. The program format calls for me, as host, to ask the first question.

On the way from my office on the third floor of the Rayburn Building to the House Recording Studio several floors below, I thought about what my opening question should be. One of my staff aides had suggested that I ask Bolling if he blamed defeat of his reform plan on his fellow Democrats, who voted overwhelmingly against it. I vetoed this suggestion not only because it was a little harsh, but also because Dick Bolling is a good Democrat who does not make a practice of hurling bricks at his own party. I decided to phrase the question in general terms.

"Are you," I asked as the tape began to roll, "satisfied with the changes in procedures voted recently by the House?"

"Of course not," Bolling replied without a trace of hesitation. "I wasn't the least bit pleased when a majority of my own party turned on (my) bill and managed to scuttle the major parts of it."

Bolling explained it precisely as it had been: "A majority of the Republicans voted for the good version (of reform) and a majority of Democrats voted for the bad one."

Sometimes partisanship expects too much of honest men like Dick Bolling.

The Bolling Plan: What It Tried to Solve

The committee system in the U.S. House of Representatives is a hopelessly chaotic maze of overlapping jurisdictions, obsolete mandates and unholy alliances. It is tired. It is old. It is insane.

Energy is a perfect example of the kind of problem that the present committee system is incapable of dealing with effectively. Only in recent years has energy become an issue deemed worthy of congressional attention. Since it was not a major issue in 1946, when the present committee system was set up, the jurisdiction is vague. When energy became a big issue in the 1970s, the system was unable to respond.

It is entirely conceivable that the leadership could sit down and say: "This energy issue is a big problem that requires real action. Let's decide who is going to be responsible for getting a program off the ground." Unfortunately, however, Members of Congress are not built that way. Everyone wants a piece of the energy action because it's one of the most exciting and important issues going. Ambitious committee chairmen and subcommittee chairmen stumble and fall over one another like drunken sailors fighting for a favorable position. As a result, nothing gets done.

At the present time there are a total of 33 committees and 65 subcommittees of Congress that claim some jurisdiction over the Energy Research and Development Administration (the agency established by Congress to oversee development of new sources of energy). They hold hearings, listen to testimony, call press conferences and write reports. Mountains of paper. Lots of noise. And no action.

Between January and August of 1975, Administration officials testified before 86 separate Hill panels. They made 344 appearances during that eight-month period and gave 732 hours of testimony based on an estimated 15,000 hours of preparation that included meetings, briefings, drafts and memoranda. All of this goes on at the public expense, of course.

Energy is by no means an isolated example of how progress on important issues is thwarted by an obsolete system of congressional committees. Education is another.

There are 22 standing committees in the House of Representatives. Eighteen of them have some jurisdiction over education. Education is the business of at least 70 congressional subcommittees. Collectively, they have given birth to some 439 federal programs administered by more than 50 federal agencies that relate to post-secondary education alone. Is it any wonder that we lack a coherent education policy at the national level of government?

Fortunately, it is becoming better known that Congress is the main culprit for refusing to put its own house in order. Still, a veto of an education bill (or health bill, or social security increase, etc.), is bound to be unpopular, regardless of the justification. In the case of the education appropriations bill for fiscal year 1976, the President had decided that several programs such as the Impact Aid program required far too much money and were far too poorly administered to merit his support. I decided that I would support the President's veto, even though I knew that school officials in Arizona and elsewhere would not look too kindly on my position.

A few days before the scheduled vote on the President's veto, I received a telephone call from one of the leading figures in the Arizona Education Association. After some initial pleasantries, the man said to me: "You know, John, I can't say this publicly, and I'll deny saying it if you repeat it to anyone, but that education bill should have been vetoed. The money isn't going where we need it to go. It's about time someone said no."

The country has no comprehensive education, energy or health policy because Congress is structurally incapable of producing it. The system worked well when it was first established and for some time after that. But a system can only go so long without repairs, particularly now in the face of the growing complexity of our problems.

The Bolling plan proposed a major re-structuring of House committee jurisdictions. Its suggestions included the consolidation of health-related programs in the Interstate and Foreign Commerce Committee (to be renamed Commerce and Health); transfer of research and development programs, now scattered among five separate committees, to a new Science and Technology Committee; the concentration of transportation programs in a new Public Works and Transportation Committee; the transformation of the Interior and

Insular Affairs Committee into an Energy and Environment Committee; and much more.

The Bolling plan also proposed some important institutional reforms, chief among them a provision to limit each Member of the House to service on just one standing committee. This would have enabled each Member to concentrate his or her energies in one area, encouraging the development of a degree of expertise that would upgrade the quality of legislative proposals. As it is now, Members of Congress are spread far too thin; they shuttle between committees and subcommittees that frequently hold hearings simultaneously. During the past 20 years, the workload borne by each Member has increased many times over, as has the complexity of the issues he is expected to help solve. But the system has remained basically unchanged. While the challenges of the job have increased, the tools have remained the same. The Bolling plan was aimed at forging new tools for new tasks.

The Bolling Plan: Who Killed It?

A list of the individuals who played parts in the destruction of the single most extensive congressional reform effort since 1946 reads like a 'who's who' in the Democratic power structure. With the exception of Speaker Albert—who stuck loyally by the Bolling plan to the end but could not control the Caucus—most of the Democratic heavyweights viewed the plan not as reform, but as a direct threat to their own power.

Committee chairmen are a strange breed. They are treated with great deference and respect by all Members of the House and are always addressed as "Mr. Chairman". They enjoy benefits not afforded ordinary Members, such as additional staff, travel allowances and office space.

They are attracted to power like moths to a flame. They jealously rule their respective committees as fiefdoms within an ancient feudal system and are powerful overlords to whom prestige is more important than legislative productivity.

There are many able and entirely competent committee chairmen. But they are not likely to agree on any changes in procedure that will result in a loss of their personal responsibility or power. On the contrary, they can be expected to fight like tigers to preserve the status quo.

Wilbur Mills, a once powerful chairman of the House Ways and Means Committee, is a typical example. The Bolling plan earned Mills' wrath because it proposed to transfer from Ways and Means all but the tax aspects of foreign trade, health, unemployment compensation and general revenue sharing. The Bolling plan also made it mandatory that all standing committees operate with at least four subcommittees in order to preserve jurisdictional integrity and reduce committee workloads. Mills had never operated with subcommittees. He had always insisted on running the entire show himself, and he was not about to change his ways at this late stage.

John Dingell of Michigan, who was to become a key figure in the energy debate, turned on the Bolling plan when he realized that it would gut the power of a subcommittee of the Merchant Marine and Fisheries Committee which he chaired. Using a twisted bit of logic, Dingell accused the Members of the Bolling panel of operating out of "self-interest."

"A careful analysis . . . will reveal that they (Bolling Committee Members) are either . . . retiring or, second running for some other office," Dingell said on the House Floor.

Ralph Nader came out against the Bolling Plan. Given his reputation as a leading consumer advocate, as well as his interest in the legislative process, it was surprising to many of us that Nader would want to oppose the most important reform effort in over a quarter of a century. But he did, and his opposition most certainly had an effect on the attitudes of many Democratic Members. Nader argued that energy and environment were individually too important to be linked together in one committee, as prescribed under the Bolling

Plan. Nader got his way . . . but today Congress has neither an energy committee nor an environment committee.

The most damaging fusillade came from organized labor. Labor was dead set against the Bolling plan because it would have split the Labor and Education Committee into two major committees, each with separate jurisdictions. Labor and education have always been an unnatural pair. However, they were linked in 1946 because of the relatively small workload confronting them both. Since that time, the role of labor in America has drastically increased, as has the scope of federal involvement in education. A change was definitely in order.

Why did organized labor object to the proposed split? For the simple reason that it had quite successfully invested years of time, money and hard work into stacking certain committees with liberals receptive to its own views. The 26 Democrats on the Education and Labor Committee, for example, received a total of more than $400,000 in campaign contributions from labor in 1974. For 21 of them, the labor money represented 10% or more of their total campaign treasury. Seven Members received more than $20,000 apiece and 11 Members were handed contributions of $10,000 to $20,000. Obviously, these Members find it very difficult to vote contrary to the wishes of labor and they can usually be counted on to respond affirmatively to labor-backed proposals, as they did in 1975 by voting out the Common Situs Picketing bill.

Labor forces put out the word that the Bolling plan was unacceptable. Ready to answer their call was one of the greatest liberal soldiers in the House, Phillip Burton. A key Democrat on the Education and Labor Committee, Burton had everything to lose and nothing to gain from the Bolling plan. He jumped into the fracas with enthusiasm.

Burton received help from Wayne Hays, another Democrat with nothing to gain and much to lose from reform. Hays objected to the reform plan on the self-serving grounds that it would remove jurisdiction over campaign election and finance laws from his House Administration Committee and shift it to the bipartisan Committee on Standards of Official Conduct. This was another long overdue change. A definite conflict of interest is involved when a committee controlled by the majority party sets out to construct laws aimed at treating all parties fairly.

The conflict of interest was exacerbated by the dual role of Wayne Hays himself. In March, 1974, the nonpartisan Common Cause took out a full page advertisement in the *Washington Post* which proclaimed: "There's Another Political Scandal in Town, But This One Belongs To The Democrats."

"Is it not a scandal," Common Cause asked, "that Wayne Hays, the man responsible in 1974 for the Democratic Congressional Campaign fund raising and money dispensing is also the man responsible for writing legislation to reform campaign finance practices?"

Wayne Hays didn't see it that way. In typical fashion, he took to the House Floor to denounce the ad and its author, "Common *Curse*."

Burton and Hays worked diligently to line up opponents to the Bolling plan. Their effort received its acid test on May 9, 1974, when the Caucus met to determine a course of action. Before the Caucus was a motion made by Burton to refer the Bolling plan to a Caucus subcommittee. Burton insisted that the vote be taken by secret ballot, a clever move because it guaranteed the Democrats complete anonymity. The secret ballot ensured passage of the Burton motion and the eventual defeat of the Bolling plan.

The Caucus subcommittee headed by the respected Washington Congresswoman Julia Butler Hansen did come up with some improvements in the system, but not the overhaul it needs. The major provisions of the Bolling plan were discarded. The one-Member-per-committee provision was thrown out. Education and Labor remain together. Energy jurisdiction is still nonexistent.

In the face of public pressure for reform, some had hoped

Haunted House

Haunted House—from **Herblock's State of the Union** (Simon & Shuster, 1972)

the Hansen panel might rise to the occasion and propose serious changes. However, they had only to glance at the names on the panel in order to be disappointed. Heading the list were none other than Phillip J. Burton and Wayne L. Hays.

In the Democratic Congress, the cards had been stacked against meaningful reform from the beginning.

Why did a majority of House Democrats band together to kill the Bolling plan? Probably the best explanation was provided by Majority Leader Tip O'Neill. "Reform," Tip explained, "is like cutting the budget and taxes. You're for it until it affects your own district. With this reform, the name of the game is power and the boys don't want to give it up."

Precisely the point. Why should anyone expect Members of a twenty year-old majority to give up their power? Why should they be different from anyone else?

Members of Congress are no worse than most people. They want to do a good job. They care about the Nation's problems. But, like most people, they often tend to place themselves first. They are ambitious and strive to achieve power and influence. When they do achieve a measure of personal success and status, they naturally cling to it with all their strength.

It is simply unrealistic to expect a chairman of a congressional committee or subcommittee, or an officer of the majority leadership, to go along with any changes in the system that would diminish his power, no matter how well-reasoned the arguments for change might be.

Genuine congressional reform will not take place until the American people place control of Congress in the hands of another political party.

The Democrats will never agree to the kinds of reform that are needed because a system that has served them well over the years would have to be changed. It is the self-interest factor, powerful and pervasive, that stands in the way of real reform.

Not even the last large and enthusiastic crop of Democratic freshmen could force the sort of changes that are needed. They came to Washington determined to have an impact. They succeeded in removing three committee chairmen, but that was only a superficial change and not a basic reform. Congress continues to conduct the public's business in the confused and ineffective manner of the past. Significantly, a survey conducted towards the end of the First Session of the 94th Congress by the polling firm of William R. Hamilton and Staff indicated that most people do not believe that the freshmen have had any success in reforming or improving Congress. The Democratic freshmen learned a hard fact of congressional life: power resides in the hands of the majority leadership, and if the leadership is opposed to change, change will not occur.

The American people should realize that congressional reform cannot be accomplished by the majority party. The ins have little incentive to change. It is the outs—the powerless minority—who have the only real motivation to take a critical look at the system and determine a better way to run things.

When the people change party control of Congress, both the people and Congress will benefit greatly. The reforms to which the minority committed itself during its period of isolation will occur. The system will change; it will really change. Then, as years pass and new problems of unforeseen origin and complexity arise, the system will require change once more. As before, the majority will find itself unable to respond. Then they will have to be replaced.

It is the periodic switching of party control that will result in a Congress which keeps itself institutionally fit.

6   The Road to a Better Congress

"A Republican Congress would know where it wanted to go, and how to get there."
—John J. Rhodes, *September 8, 1975*

IMAGINE that it is January, 1977. The House of Representatives has come together for the start of the 95th Congress. The galleries are packed with the families and friends of the Members, as well as many curious spectators from all across the land. On the House Floor, I mount the rostrum and prepare to assume my duties as the newly-elected Speaker of the House. I take the gavel from my good friend Carl Albert, who has been elected Minority Leader, commend him for the work he has done in the past, and request that all Members put partisanship aside to work together in the national interest. The applause is loud and long.

Fantasy? I call it an optimistic expectation. At any rate, there would be little question as to what a Republican Congress would do. The scenario has already been laid out in the Republican Legislative Agenda.

The House Republican Legislative Agenda was developed in 1975 to give the people an incentive to elect Republicans to Congress. The Agenda, authored by a cross section of GOP House Members, identifies the basic legislative goals of a Republican-controlled Congress. It is positive and forward looking. Parts of it are innovative. And it offers a way out of America's present big government doldrums.

There were hazards involved in its initial development. The chief danger was the implication that House Republicans were suggesting dissatisfaction with President Ford's program. No congressional party in history had ever put together a legislative program of its own with a sitting President of the same party in the White House. Traditionally, the President proposes a legislative program and his party in Congress rubber-stamps it. By developing a separate program, House Republicans were breaking a long tradition.

I chose to take the risks involved in breaking tradition for two reasons.

First, I staunchly believe that both congressional parties ought to have an image of their own that is readily distinguishable from the image of the President or of presidential aspirants. During non-presidential election years, I think that the national party emphasis ought to be on the congressional party. The American public has long been mesmerized by the presidency and the men who seek it. By comparison, other branches and levels of government receive only cursory attention. I much prefer a situation in which all areas of government receive scrutiny by the voters . . . not just the Executive.

The idea for a Republican Legislative Agenda separate from the White House was part of an ongoing effort to get the American people to "think Congress."

The second reason for putting together a House Republican program of our own had to do with my belief that the days of presidential coattails are gone forever. In 1952, Barry Goldwater and I were carried into office from the Democratic state of Arizona mainly on the strength of Dwight David Eisenhower's enormous popularity. So too were many other Republican candidates. As far as I can tell, that marked the end of the coattail era in American politics. Four year later, for example, General Eisenhower won another landslide victory; yet Republicans failed to recapture control of the House and Senate which had been lost in 1954. In 1972, Richard Nixon was re-elected President by the largest majority in history; yet Republicans picked up a mere handful of congressional seats. As a matter of fact, there probably now exists a reverse coattail effect in American politics as was demonstrated in the 1974 elections when Republican congressional candidates were punished at the polls for the sins of a Republican President.

The Republican Party has controlled the White House for 14 of the last 22 years but has run Congress for only two years during that same period, which clearly demonstrates that it is possible for popular candidates to be elected President without their party capturing control of Congress. Republican candidates for Congress cannot get elected by being tails on someone else's kite. If control of Congress is ever to be wrested from the Democrats, it is up to congressional Republicans to tell our own story to the people.

Where Are We Now?

The first priority of a Republican-controlled Congress will be to determine the exact status of the existing programs of Government. Accordingly, there will be no new federal programs enacted during our first session. Regular appropriations bills, of course, will be adopted through procedures established by the new Budget and Impoundment Control Act. Congress will respond to emergency problems with appropriate legislative remedies. But new programs will all be placed on hold during our first year in control.

A do-nothing Congress? On the contrary, the first session will be very busy. At long last, Congress will be hard at work fulfilling a responsibility that has been sadly neglected for quite some time. Congress will work on oversight!

Oversight, as I explained earlier, is intensive review by Congress of enacted laws and programs to determine (a) whether the original intent of Congress is being fulfilled and (b) whether changing events have justified the continuation of the program as well as the cost increases.

John Gardner of Common Cause has called it the "liberal illusion" to regard federal aid as the only key to national problem-solving. "When in doubt," Gardner described the typical liberal Democratic response, "spend more dollars, pile program on program. Too little attention has been paid to whether these programs are fulfilling their purposes."

Every year, Congress has enacted more new programs and more federal regulations. These programs and regulations do not self-destruct after a few years. They live on *ad infinitum,* increasing in both cost and complexity. It is not unusual— in fact it is quite normal—for a given program, five or six years following its birth, to bear very little resemblance to its original shape.

As an example, let us say that a Member of the House arrives on the Floor for a vote on "H.R. 1," a bill to establish an "inner-city public parks agency." Unless he worked on the bill in committee, chances are that the Congressman is unfamiliar with the details. He therefore asks a colleague or a Floor attendant at least two questions. One of them is: "What does the bill do?" He is told that it creates a new federal agency to search for locations within the inner-city suitable for conversion into public parks. The agency will oversee the development of these parks and hand down regulations concerning their maintenance and use.

The Congressman will also ask: "How much does the program cost?" He is told that the parks agency is budgeted at a level of $80 million during its first year of operation. The Member may feel that $80 million is a small price for such a noble and worthwhile program, particularly since we spend many billions of dollars on defense. He decides to vote aye, is joined by a majority of his colleagues and the bill later becomes public law.

The problems arise several years later. That well-intentioned public parks program, tagged originally with a price of only $80 million, now costs the taxpayers over a billion dollars a year! To make matters worse, the program no longer performs the function Congress originally intended. New administrators and new personnel have twisted the original intent of the legislation. Local officials even complain that regulations handed down by the agency discourage the development of parks within the inner city.

In short, what started out as a positive modest program is, six years later, expensive and ineffective. Yet the program remains in existence and its administrators hand down counterproductive rules and regulations, harass local officials and cost the taxpayers of the country huge amounts of money. Why? Because Congress has refused to make the effort to look back and check on the program's performance. Congress has neglected its responsibility to conduct oversight.

The "inner-city public parks agency" is a hypothetical example of federal bureaucracy gone awry. Another example, the Food Stamp program, is real—too real. Between 1961 and 1964, the Food Stamp program was a test project. Food stamps were distributed to 367,000 needy persons at a cost of $66 million. The program's early performance was so good that President Lyndon Johnson made it a permanent fixture in his Great Society and Congress enacted it into public law in late 1964.

Few will quarrel with the basic idea behind food stamps: to provide some of our real farm surpluses to the hungry. But,

like many other well-intentioned federal programs, the Food Stamp program soon expanded its function, relaxed its eligibility standards, and invited abuse. The concept may have been noble, but the manner of execution caused a fiasco.

Today, the Food Stamp program is operating in 3,046 locations nationwide as well as in Puerto Rico, Guam and the Virgin Islands. In November, 1975, the caseload stood at 18.8 million persons, up 5,300% from November, 1964. The program cost a total of $4.7 billion in fiscal 1975—a 15,300% increase over its original budget.

If left untouched, the Food Stamp program will continue to grow with reckless abandon. The Office of Management and Budget estimates that $7.3 billion will be spent on food stamps during fiscal year 1977. That's more than one-half of the entire budget of the U.S. Department of Agriculture! The caseload will rise to 22.5 million persons. It is estimated that up to one-half of our entire population is currently eligible under the present regulations to receive food stamps from the Government.

As if eligibility standards were not lax enough, a significant number of ineligible Americans deliberately take advantage of the program. During the first six months of 1975, according to the Agriculture Department, about 929,000 people received some $19.4 million in food stamp benefits to which they were not entitled.

Other programs have followed a similar pattern. It is important that the American people realize that three-fourths of all federal spending is mandated. Most of the more than 1,000 programs on the books have built-in escalators and obligations. Regardless of how ineffective a program may be, the law is there and Congress must either rewrite it or fund the program as planned. Congress mainly takes the easy route by automatically funding existing programs without checking to see where the money is actually going.

As was pointed out by Donald Lambro, a Washington reporter: "We have given the Bedouins $17,000 for a dry cleaning plant to clean their djellabas. We studied the smell of perspiration from Australian aborigines for a mere $70,000. We've spent $15,000 to study Yugoslavian lizards, $71,000 to compile a history of comic books, $5,000 to analyze violin varnish, $19,300 to determine why children fall off tricycles, and $375,000 for the Pentagon to study frisbees." [11] These are relatively minor examples of federal expenditures of questionable legitimacy. But multiplied many times by the lengthy number of similar expenditures, the amount of annual governmental waste—and the degree of corresponding congressional neglect—becomes truly unconscionable.

By devoting its first year entirely to congressional oversight, a Republican Congress will attempt to weed out programs that no longer serve useful purposes and cut back on spending enormous sums that are not justified. We will take a major step towards reducing the huge automatic increases that now push the federal budget inexorably higher every passing year.

Is a Balanced Budget Possible?

Republicans cling to the common sense notion that the federal Government should spend only as much as it takes in. We equate the federal budget to the budget of the average American family. A family can get away with spending beyond its means for a while. Eventually, however, overspending is bound to take its toll. Credit will be withheld. Confidence will be shaken and fiscal chaos will ensue.

The Democrats don't seem to care too much about federal budgets that are unbalanced. "Fiscal responsibility" has always been a dirty phrase to them, for it implies that there are some things that Government cannot do because of fiscal restraints. The Democrats do not like to hear that kind of talk. They like to believe that Government can do anything it wants to do, regardless of the financial realities. Only in recent months, when opinion polls have shown the American public's disenchantment with reckless spending policies, have the Democrats suddenly professed concern with the size of the federal budget.

The growth of the federal budget literally defies belief. It took the United States 174 years to reach a budget of $100 billion. But in just nine years, Congress doubled that figure. Four years later, the $300 billion mark was crossed. We will probably have a budget in excess of $400 billion in fiscal year 1977, President Ford's efforts to hold it down to $394.2 billion notwithstanding.

This enormous spending binge has absolutely no relation to population growth. In 1929 we had 120 million Americans and a budget of $3 billion. Today there are around 215 million Americans and we have a budget in excess of $365 billion. During a period when the American population has grown 77%, federal spending has skyrocketed nearly 12,000%.

A good chunk of the money we have spent is money that we do not have. Thirty-five years ago, the Government had a national debt of $42 billion. Today the debt is $577 billion. These huge deficits have sapped the nation's economic strength.

Because Congress must appropriate every cent in the budget, Congress bears the major responsibility for the budgetary mess facing America. Congress must take the lead to restore a semblance of fiscal sanity. Congress must commit itself to achieving a balanced budget.

This is precisely the commitment a Republican Congress is prepared to make. We recognize, of course, that transition from a yearly deficit of $80 billion to budgetary balance in the space of just one year is unrealistic. So we have set a three-year spending de-escalation deadline, within which time the budget will be balanced.

The balancing of outlays with revenues will require some tough budgetary decisions. They will not be made at the expense of people with special problems. I am convinced that fiscal responsibility and human compassion are entirely compatible. The Government can have a heart without losing its head in the process.

Halting the federally-fueled spiral of inflation will produce more jobs, higher spendable income and more economic security over the years ahead.

We believe that this is the kind of fiscal responsibility the American people want and the country needs.

How To Find More Jobs?

A major cause of unemployment is the ever-changing nature of the marketplace. Jobs in a given area which once were plentiful are no longer available. There may be jobs available in other areas, but the unemployed worker never hears about them or often finds that he or she is unqualified to fill them. The jobless person becomes one of the permanently unemployed despite a strong desire to work.

The Democrats share our desire to put the unemployed back to work. But they use the wrong approach. They say they want to create jobs, but give scant attention to the kinds of jobs created and their long-range effect on both the individual and the economy.

The basic Democratic approach is to enact legislation that creates large numbers of so-called public service jobs. Such jobs, usually of the leaf-raking variety, may shift people off the welfare rolls but do little to make the individual feel that he is a meaningful member of society. They also do nothing to stimulate production in the private sector where real jobs are to be found. The Democratic solution is really no solution at all; it is just a stopgap.

A Republican Congress will use a different approach. We will enact a program of automatically extended unemployment benefits, coupled with a system of intensive manpower training. Under this plan, the unemployed worker will receive compensation from the Government up to a certain point in time. At the end of that time, if a job opportunity in his previous line of work is not forthcoming, he will be given a chance to retrain in another vocation or skill of his choice, as well as special counseling to locate a job for him in his new profession.

In other words, we will take even better care of the person who is unemployed. But we won't just leave him. We will go out and try to find him another job and provide him with the skills necessary to qualify for it. We will bring workers and jobs together.

It seems to me that this common-sense approach is definitely superior to Democratic leaf-raking. In the first place, it will give people jobs from which they can derive a reasonable degree of fulfillment. Second, it represents a practical way of adapting the work force to the ever-changing character of the marketplace. It is different. It is innovative. I think it represents one workable and effective answer to the serious problem of joblessness in America.

After Retirement—What?

Social security has proved inadequate to meet the financial needs of many Americans who have reached retirement age. When the program was originally started, it was not intended to serve as the sole source of income for older Americans, but only as a supplement to other sources. Yet the simple fact is that social security is now expected to be the principal means of support for millions of elderly Americans.

To ensure this vital source of income the integrity of the Social Security Trust Fund must be preserved. Extended coverage, expansion of benefits and cost of living escalators have combined to place great pressures on the Fund. It is not growing at the present time. Benefits have far outdistanced payments, causing a real crisis for the future. According to the Office of Management and Budget, unfunded future

Editorial cartoon by Don Hesse. Copyright, **St. Louis Globe Democrat.** Reprinted with permission of the Los Angeles Times Syndicate.

obligations for social security total $2.7 trillion. At this writing, there is only enough in the Social Security Trust Fund to pay for eight months of benefits at the current rate. We cannot continue to raise payroll taxes to pay for social security because the tax burden on the worker is already severe. The only other available alternative would be to finance social security through the general revenue. This plan is also unacceptable for it would change social security from an insurance program to a straight welfare program. Obviously, Congress must develop a whole new method of financing the fund . . . and soon.

But more is needed. Congress must devise some means of providing people with a way of augmenting Social Security benefits. We think we have an answer.

A Republican Congress will enact an extended Keogh-type plan to provide special tax incentives for workers to invest in their own private retirement fund. Savings from such funds will eventually be used to supplement both social security and company pension plans.

This approach will represent far more than simply saving for the future because the generous tax advantages derived from contributing to a retirement fund will benefit the American worker and his family as he invests. With a little planning, the American citizen can gauge just how much money he and his family will need during retirement and contribute to the fund accordingly.

This plan will help solve another problem—America's need for a vast amount of capital formation. What is capital formation? Very simply, it is the cash money saved by people— the capital—which is needed by business and industry to expand production and create more jobs. It takes money to build a new plant or to open a new branch office, and it is the opening of a new plant or a new office that represents new job opportunities for people.

A good estimate is that we must invest more than $4 trillion in new facilities over the coming decade in order to absorb the 1½ million Americans who enter the labor force each year as well as to maintain the 85 million already working. We will need every possible source of investment capital to meet this great need.

By establishing an individual retirement fund and contributing to it regularly, the individual American will build his own security and help his country towards a growing and prosperous economic future. It is a good plan that makes good sense for America.

Changing the Rules

It has been a major contention of this book that today's Congress lacks the tools needed to perform effectively. The system is old and has gone too long without repair to be responsive.

Therefore, in order to make it possible to enact the issue-oriented proposals contained in the Republican Legislative Agenda, a Republican Congress will move to bring the legislative branch into the twentieth century.

The House Republican Task Force on Reform was established in 1974 to study the rules and procedures of the House of Representatives and suggest needed changes. Since we do not have the votes at the present time to enact the proposals that emerged, one of our goals was to prod the majority in the right direction. We are proud that some of the Task Force's recommendations, such as open committee meetings and lifting of the Caucus unit rule, have been adopted, at least in part, by the Democrats.

The report of the Task Force is also meant to give the people an idea of what Republicans would change were they in control of the legislative branch. The Task Force, which was ably headed by Congressman Bill Frenzel of Minnesota, operated under the auspices of the House Republican Research Committee. It bears the imprimatur of the Republican leadership.

The final report of the Task Force on Reform is reprinted in its entirety in the Appendix. I have selected a few random points for the purpose of examination here.

An important adjunct to the recently adopted rule making all committee meetings open to the public is the Republican proposal that all committee records be easily accessible to the public. Not too many people have either the time or energy to sit through an entire series of congressional hearings from beginning to end. Even the media has a hard time covering all of the many committee and subcommittee hearings.

The full committee record must be made available to the public so that the public may know how legislative decisions are made, as well as the true roles of the various participants. Many key committee decisions are made without a recorded vote. Therefore, a complete record of committee proceedings offers the one sure way in which to follow the course of a bill through the legislative process.

We also strongly believe that any Member should be able to demand a vote in committee on any question. Some committees have provisions requiring that a minimum number of Members be present before a recorded vote can take place. This is wrong and will be changed.

The Republican Task Force on Reform also addresses the critical area of congressional oversight. The commitment of a Republican Congress to legislative oversight has already been emphasized. As I have said, so serious has been the Democrats' neglect of this important duty that we will devote the first session of our first Congress almost entirely to oversight. Subsequent Republican Congresses will follow a more regularized oversight procedure.

1. All standing committees will file a report at the start of each Congress to the Committee on Government Operations

detailing their plans for legislative oversight.

2. The Government Operations Committee will serve as the oversight watchdog of all other committees of the House. If a committee neglects its oversight responsibilities, Government Operations will be expected to call this failure to the attention of the full House. Moreover, if the Government Operations Committee develops pertinent information during its own oversight, it will report on such material when related legislation is under consideration by another committee of the House.

3. All open-ended, federal grant-in-aid programs will be thoroughly reviewed every four years. This is actually required by the Intergovernmental Cooperation Act of 1968, but the Democratic Congress has not complied with the law. In order to ensure full compliance, a Republican Congress will automatically terminate every program that does not undergo the mandatory four-year review.

One important reform enacted by a Republican Congress will be to place control of the Government Operations Committee, the oversight watchdog, permanently in the hands of the minority party. In a Republican Congress, the chairman of Government Operations will be a Democrat; in a Democratic Congress (unless the rules were changed back) the chairman will be a Republican. This will represent an important check on the majority that is currently missing. It will force the majority to exercise fully its oversight responsibility and ensure a better, more modern government.

Republicans supported the jurisdictional changes recommended by the Select Committee on Committees in its 1973 report and would act to realign jurisdictions in a Republican-controlled Congress. Recognizing, however, that a Republican Congress is a thing of the future, we will set up some sort of a bipartisan (equal membership) panel to review the then existing committee structure and recommend any needed reforms. The Bolling plan will serve as a good starting point.

I have personally also advocated creation of a Select Committee on Energy to end once and for all the jurisdictional confusion that now prevents real energy progress. The Select Committee would have sole jurisdiction over energy legislation before the House. As Speaker, I will do what is necessary to incorporate this idea into the committee realignment plan.

Finally, a Republican Congress will limit each Member to service on just one major committee at a time. The importance of this proposal cannot be emphasized enough. As it is now, the average House Member sits on two standing committees, and can be assigned to as many as four or five subcommittees. Because most committees and subcommittees hold hearings in the morning before the House convenes, a Member's time and attention is obviously spread dangerously thin. Some of the more energetic and conscientious Members try to make an appearance at simultaneously scheduled hearings. But there is very little chance for concentrated study.

Woodrow Wilson correctly observed that "Congress in its committee rooms is Congress at work." The fact that most Members of Congress are forced by the sheer size of the committee system to neglect major aspects of committee work is one of the chief causes of the inferior legislation before Congress in recent years. The limitation of one-committee-assignment-per-Member will solve this problem.

Implicit in this proposal, of course, is the necessity of reducing the overall number of committees. Reduction is a very positive development that will consolidate committee jurisdictions and streamline the entire legislative process.

Because they can be mailed under the congressional frank, the Member's signature which takes the place of postage, newsletters can be delivered to each and every household in a Member's district, enabling the Member to reach many otherwise unreachable people with his or her message. When used responsibly, they can be an entirely worthwhile public service. When misused, they represent campaign propaganda at the taxpayers' expense.

Some Members, such as my colleague from Arizona, Morris Udall, have distinguished themselves by putting out high quality newsletters that inform the public. Other Members, such as former Democratic Congressman Frank Clark of Pennsylvania, have gone to great lengths in the opposite direction. Clark was defeated in 1974 by Republican Gary Myers. Yet in early 1975, the people of Pennsylvania's 25th District received a newsletter from "Your Congressman, Frank Clark," as if nothing had happened in November. Since former Members of Congress are entitled to use the franking privilege for a period following their term, Clark was able to send out a newsletter without having to pay postage. The Clark newsletter contained a discussion of various issues, and a telephone number in Washington where he could be reached. It was as if he had never been defeated!

The franking privilege carries with it some rather strict requirements concerning what kind of mail can be sent out at the taxpayers' expense. The House Post Office and Civil Service committee has jurisdiction over the congressional franking privilege and maintains strict requirements as to its use. All official congressional business can be conducted via the frank. All self-promotional (news releases, etc.) or partisan mailings (campaign brochures, etc.) require postage. Since the frankability of any mail is subject to challenge, some Members, myself included, obtain the frankability judgment of the Post Office and Civil Service Committee before preparing large mailings.

Since postage costs are nonexistent for Members of Congress, the main consideration in the preparation of congressional newsletters is the cost of printing which can be considerable. [The typical mailing I put out costs approximately $2,500.] Some Members pay for their newsletters out of public relations funds set up by their respective congressional com-

"STOP WORRYING ABOUT THE BRAKES"

Editorial cartoon by Don Hesse. Copyright, **St. Louis Globe Democrat.** Reprinted with permission of the Los Angeles Times Syndicate.

mittees; others pay for them out of pocket; still others set up special funds that are financed by friendly individuals and organizations.

The Democratic majority in the 94th Congress made it much easier to finance the printing of expensive newsletters. Over strenuous Republican objections, Wayne Hays' House Administration committee gave each Member an annual sum of $5,000 to spend on printed communications. The motivation for creation of this generous newsletter allowance was the realization of the Democratic leadership that most of the new Democratic freshmen would face tough elections in 1976. Since district mailings are a powerfully effective communications medium, the Democratic leadership gave their freshmen some sorely needed help—all at the taxpayers' expense! This is but one example of how the Democrats have worked with great success to construct an incumbent protection system. Because of the considerable financial resources available to incumbents, most of whom are Democrats, it is very difficult for a Republican challenger to mount an effective campaign.

A Republican Congress will abolish the $5,000 annual newsletter allowance on the grounds that it is an unnecessary public expense. We will also require full and complete disclosure of the source of all funds used by Members to finance their newsletters. Finally, we will limit the maximum size of any contribution to a Member's newsletter fund to $1,000 per individual and prohibit corporations and labor unions from making contributions.

The Republican Task Force on Reform is adamant in its opposition to proxy voting, the procedure whereby a Member of Congress can vote in committee or subcommittee without really being present at the time of the vote. Proxy voting enables Members to give the appearance of participating in committee work without actually doing so. It also enables committee chairmen and other powerful committee members to overrule the judgment of Members who performed their committee work diligently by controlling the proxies of those Members who may never have shown up for hearings.

Actually, we thought that we had won the fight to do away with proxy voting. For on October 8, 1974, the House voted in favor of an amendment to the Hansen reform bill to ban its use. Three months later, in the secrecy of the Caucus, the Democrats reversed that decision and thus offered another example of how dangerous the Democratic Caucus can be. Aware of the fact that the public and the press are watching Floor activity, the Democrats will frequently go along with a popular motion, such as a ban on proxy voting. Then, when no one is looking, they quietly retreat to the protection of the Caucus and completely frustrate the will of the full House. Thus does "King Caucus" rule supreme, unwatched, unchecked.

Proxy voting is wrong. It helps to perpetuate a Congress in which lazy and irresponsible Members can trick the people into believing that they are working hard on their behalf. It will be eliminated once and for all by a Republican Congress.

A Republican Congress will insist that the *Congressional Record* be a completely accurate chronicle of all that takes place in Congress. We will move swiftly to end all practices that currently contribute to a distorted picture of legislative activity.

One of the changes we will institute is a requirement that any words inserted into the *Record* by a Member but not spoken on the Floor, appear in a distinguishably different type. Should a Member desire to have his remarks included in the body of an actual debate, but not care to deliver them personally, his statement will appear at the end of the debate in distinguishably different type. In a Republican Congress, there will be no confusion as to who said what, and when.

We will also eliminate much of the extraneous matter unrelated to legislative or public policy issues which invariably appears in the *Record*. Every time a Member of Congress inserts a page of print into the *Record,* it costs the American taxpayer $286.00. There are often hundreds of pages of extraneous material in each day's *Record,* and the resultant cost becomes considerable. We will cut this cost.

Finally, in addition to the printed version of the *Congressional Record,* Republicans will insure that the public will have easy access to the unedited record of all that transpires on the House Floor.

Democratic leaders have been reluctant to permit live media coverage of Floor proceedings on the grounds that it would disrupt the normal flow of legislative business. Republicans believe that the objections raised against media coverage are not sufficient to prevent the people, via the media, from seeing and hearing their Congress at work. A Republican Congress will remove the current restrictions on such coverage.

The argument against media coverage most frequently heard is that the presence of television cameras is likely to encourage some of the more flamboyant Members to engage in showmanship at the expense of the business before the House. There will always be Members who rise on the Floor simply because each is in love with the sound of his own voice. They can be counted on to perform with or without television cameras.

The impeachment hearings of the House Judiciary Committee demonstrated that Members of Congress are perfectly capable of acting responsibly in the presence of television cameras. In fact, so ably did the Judiciary Committee Members conduct their business that the House voted 385 to 25 to permit live coverage of the anticipated Floor debate on impeachment. The ground rules for this coverage were worked out by the bipartisan leadership and the various network heads in a meeting held in the Speaker's office the day before President Nixon resigned.

I cannot help feeling that the real reason why the Democratic leadership bars media coverage of Floor proceedings is their fear that it will bring home to the American people just how disorganized and unresponsive the Democratic Congress can be. The Democrats are already in power and have nothing to gain from increased exposure or visibility. One sees again why reform must come from the minority.

Save for the installation of an electronic voting system in 1970, there have been few changes in either congressional structure or procedure since the Legislative Reorganization Act of 1946. Times change but Congress remains the same.

The changes advocated by the Republican minority represent the most sweeping reforms developed in 30 years. They do not represent all the answers. But there can be little doubt that our recommendations would, if enacted, result in a dramatic increase in congressional efficiency. We have studied the system carefully and have emerged with a blueprint for progress . . . a blueprint that should be adopted . . . a blueprint that <u>will</u> be adopted when Republicans are given control of the legislative branch.

7   Revise by Dissent

". . . Democrats have maintained their margins in Congress by skillful exploitation of the advantages of incumbency and the weaknesses of their Republican opposition."

—David Broder, Washington Post

FUTILITY is a relative term. One man's futility can be another man's gratification. This is especially true in politics where everything is relative.

But my feeling of futility stems from the existence of an amazing paradox. The paradox is this: An overwhelming majority of Americans condemn the performance of Democratic Congresses; yet they keep electing Democrats! It would be one thing if the voters elected Democratic Congresses because they approved of Democratic positions on the issues. But they do not. On most of the major issues before Congress in recent years, from oil decontrol to forced busing to federal spending, public opinion polls show that most Americans

105

agreed with the Republican position and disagreed with the position taken by the Democratic majority. Still, the people continue to place control of Congress in the hands of the Democratic Party.

What are the reasons for this great paradox? Why do people consistently elect Democratic Congresses of whose actions they generally disapprove?

I can think of two reasons. The first, as previously stated, is that most Americans really do not understand how Congress works. They are taught in schools that Congress is the legislative branch of government, that it has two houses, that a bill is introduced, referred to a committee, and so forth. That is usually the extent of their training. The people have conditioned themselves to viewing Congress mostly from the limited perspective of their individual Congressman, "good old Joe," that person they elect without realizing that the individual Member is mainly powerless. The real power in Congress resides with the majority leadership. And the only way to flush out that majority leadership is to change the party membership totals.

This book represents my best effort to raise the average American's level of understanding with regard to the legislative branch. I want people of both parties to know more about Congress. Knowledge is power. Once the people know what Congress is all about, they will be better equipped to do something about their dissatisfaction with its poor performance.

Another reason for the paradox is the condition of the Republican Party, what the party is and how the party is perceived by many Americans.

We Republicans have experienced a rather rude awakening. We have discovered that the image we have of ourselves does not accord with the image other people have of us. The realization was not a complete surprise because, after all, we have heard for some time that we are a party comprised mainly of fat cats who curry favor with big business. We have heard others charge that special interests are more important to us than the needs of the average citizen. But we really never believed in our heart of hearts that most people think of us that way. I never did.

They do think of us that way, however, at least a great many do. And, frankly, for those of us who thought all along that our battles on behalf of fiscal responsibility and smaller government would eventually be rewarded, the realization that many Americans regard Republicans as the bad guys has come as quite a shock.

We now know, thanks to a survey conducted by the Republican National Committee, that Republicans are regarded by many people as hard, callous, cruel and insensitive. We give the impression of not caring—and that is the worst possible image a political party can have.

Republicans, of course, do not believe that this negative image is deserved. But in politics, it's not what you are that counts; it's what people think you are.

In reality, there is little difference in the level of sensitivity and caring between the average Republican and the average Democrat. There is frequently a major difference between our respective ways of expressing concern.

The Democrats in Congress, for example, can almost always be counted on to advocate higher spending levels on such things as Medicare, Medicaid, and Social Security. They are therefore in the enviable position of being for all these genuinely worthwhile programs. Republicans, on the other hand, argue strongly that the enormous growth of the federal budget has given rise to inflationary conditions that hurt old people on fixed incomes most of all! We try to insist on an expenditure level commensurate with income to preserve the dollar's purchasing power for all Americans. So which party is really insensitive?

Our role as the congressional minority has exacerbated our already bad image. After all, it is our duty to be critical of the program put forth by the majority. We are supposed to poke holes, identify weak spots, and suggest alternatives. Not having the votes necessary to enact a program of our own, it is our responsibility as the minority to try to improve the program of the majority. This constantly places us in a negative position and negativism is something that most Americans abhor.

Many do not realize that during the years Republicans have been a congressional minority, we have frequently developed legislative substitutes to various proposals developed by the Democrats. A good example is the Labor-HEW Appropriations bill for fiscal year 1977 which President Ford vetoed because it ran a billion dollars over his budget.

However, these two departments need annual appropriations and the country needs the vital services which they provide. Republicans were cognizant of this need. Our only quarrel was with the total dollar amount to be spent during a time when we are trying to hold down the size of the budget. We were for the programs; we just didn't want to spend as much as the Democrats.

Our course of action was as follows: a substitute Labor-HEW bill was developed by Congressman Robert Michel of Illinois, the Republican Whip and a member of the Appropriations Committee. The Michel substitute was essentially a compromise between the committee bill vetoed by the President and the President's own budget. Working behind the scenes, we were able to receive strong assurances from the White House congressional liaison team that the President would sign the compromise version of the bill.

The House Republican Policy committee met the day before the House was scheduled to consider the President's veto of the committee bill. It adopted a statement urging Republican Members to vote to sustain the President's veto and then support the Michel substitute. Accordingly, most Republicans voted to sustain the veto, but the veto was overridden.

The final record shows that a majority of Democrats voted for the Labor-HEW Appropriations bills while a majority of Republicans voted against it. Nowhere in the official voting record does it show that Republicans sponsored a reasonable substitute bill. In fact, it shows Republicans in a decidedly "anti" or negative position.

This negative image can devastate Republicans. Taken to the extreme, it results in the type of attack my Democratic opponent subjected me to in the last election. Billboards scattered throughout the first congressional district of Arizona, paid for by the Democratic candidate, proclaimed: "John Rhodes Votes Against Education 70% Of The Time." It wasn't true, but it sounded terrible! Other Republicans have had to deal with similar simplistic attacks.

The longer Republicans are forced to play the negative role of the minority, the more established our negative image with the people becomes. The longer the American people see Republicans taking a "yes, but" position on issues before Congress, the less apt they will be to develop confidence in our ability to propose positive action.

The longer a political party remains in the minority, the greater become the odds against its ever gaining majority status. The main problem facing the Republican Party today is how to make a positive impression on the American people in our current negative role.

I must admit that we haven't particularly helped ourselves. As a matter of fact, the Republican Party has flunked the test of effective communication with the people of the country. We allowed ourselves years ago to be tagged with a series of negative labels and made very little effort to shake free of these labels.

The following excerpt from the first of the famous 1960 Kennedy-Nixon debates illustrates perfectly the failure of leading Republicans to rise to the defense of their party against rhetorical charges:

KENNEDY: ". . . I think the question is, What are the programs that we advocate?

What is the party record that we lead?

I come out of the Democratic Party which in this century

has produced Woodrow Wilson, and Franklin Roosevelt, and Harry Truman . . .

Mr. Nixon comes out of the Republican Party. He was nominated by it, **and it is a fact** that through most of these last 25 years the Republican leadership has opposed Federal aid for education, medical care for the aged, development of the Tennessee Valley, development of our national resources.

I think Mr. Nixon is an effective leader of his party. I hope he would grant me the same.

The question before us is: Which point of view and which party do we want to lead the United States?"

MR. SMITH (Howard K. Smith, CBS News, Moderator): "Mr. Nixon, would you like to comment on that statement?"

NIXON: "I have no comment." [12]

Mr. Nixon should have commented here as he did on countless other occasions during the course of the debates. He should have reminded Mr. Kennedy that the very first specialized federal aid to education bill in U.S. history, a pillar of the modern educational system, was urged and signed into law by President Eisenhower, a Republican. He should have pointed out that the first American President to make protection of natural resources a matter of governmental concern was the great conservationist, Theodore Roosevelt, also a Republican. He should have said many other things. Instead, the anti-Republican charges went unanswered, leaving the viewers to conclude that the charges must be correct. I am afraid that many other Republican party leaders have been guilty of the same sin of omission.

John Kennedy was a master at extolling the alleged virtues of his own party and denigrating Republicanism. At a huge street rally in downtown Phoenix, Arizona, Democrat Kennedy said:

"This State of Arizona depends upon the wise development of your natural resources, of the effective use of water. We have dams all around the United States, built as memorials to the efforts of Franklin Roosevelt and others. We have three words that are the memorials to Republican(s): 'No new starts.' " [13]

What about <u>Coolidge</u> Dam . . . or <u>Hoover</u> Dam? And there is a Roosevelt Dam. It is located very near Phoenix, on the Salt River. But it is the <u>Theodore</u> Roosevelt Dam.

These anti-Republican charges have combined with past Republican apathy to place Republicans at a very serious political disadvantage. Today we find ourselves in a position where we hesitate to say to the people "vote Republican" because to many of them, the word Republican is a dirty word. We find to our great sadness that we must often downplay our party identification and emphasize instead our ideas.

As an example, last year the national College Republican organization distributed a series of clever advertisements emphasizing several Republican congressional initiatives. The ads, which appeared in campus newspapers around the country, were designed in such a way that our party identification was withheld until the very end. The assumption was that college youths would be surprised to learn that a progressive initiative originated with the Republican Party. And they were. Many of the students who read the ads came to agree with the tag line: "Republicans. There's More To Us Than You Think."

For some time, I have toyed with the idea of proposing that the Republican Party change its name. The theory is that since many Americans support our ideas but dislike our name, we should consider changing it. It wouldn't really matter what the new name was. After all, what's in a name? It's our program and philosophy that count most.

Frankly, I've held back making this proposal formally because of my realization that the Republican rank-and-file would never go along with it. There is too much tradition associated with our name for our party members to agree to do away with it. But it is something for them to think about.

The major challenge facing the Republican Party is one of communication. It's not enough that <u>we</u> know what we stand for. We have to make an all-out effort to let the American people know it in a language that everyone can understand.

For instance, Republicans are going to have to inform more

people about the basics of the free enterprise system. The Republican Party is really the party dedicated to furthering it and making it better. Our mistake is that we assume that all people understand how the free enterprise system works. Many do not. Nor do they fully understand why and how free enterprise, in terms of the jobs it creates and the goods and services it provides, is important to them. I am very proud that in my state of Arizona the legislature passed a law a few years back to make it mandatory that every high school offer a course on the basics of the free enterprise system. Other states would be well-advised to follow Arizona's example.

In the same way, Republicans are going to have to do a better job of getting people, particularly those on the lower rungs of the economic ladder, to understand what they have to lose from a zero or no-growth philosophy. Zero growth is the rapidly spreading notion that the United States has become too large, so therefore we should cease building and expanding our industrial capacity. Once again, it is the Republican Party that is really leading the battle against stagnation. The businessman and the corporate official understand and applaud the Republican position on this issue, but do the farmer in Kansas, the housewife in Cleveland, and the black in Watts? Do they understand that zero growth will harm them most of all by sapping their purchasing power and limiting their potential? I think not.

Republicans need to talk with America; not to America. We haven't done so in many years, if indeed we ever did. We resemble Herman Melville's immortal character, Billy Budd. We are certain that we are correct, that we have sound, workable solutions to problems that must be solved. But when we open our mouths to speak, we stutter and stammer and fail to communicate.

We need to communicate exactly what it is that we stand for. We also need to communicate the difference between our approach to Government and the approach of the Democrats.

There is a major difference between the dominant trends

of the two parties. The dominant trend of the Democratic Party, the party that controls Congress, is to the left of center. Ideological labels are rarely precise, but one of the best definitions of contemporary liberalism has been provided by columnist George Will. Liberalism, according to Will, is "a breezy confidence in the ability of federal power to achieve intended effects." The adherents of this philosophy believe that there is no problem that cannot be solved by large expenditures of money. If a program fails, the typical Democratic response is that not enough money was spent in the first place. So the Democrats up the ante and overlook the possibility that the program may have failed because it was poorly conceived or poorly executed or both.

Neither party is monolithic. The Democrats have some conservative members, among them Senator Eastland of Mississippi, Congressman Joe Waggoner of Louisiana and others. But these individuals do not represent the dominant trend of their party. They are aberrants.

The dominant trend of the Republican Party is located in the middle of the ideological spectrum. Like the Democrats, we have our exceptions, such as Jacob Javits, Clifford Case and Pete McCloskey. Thank goodness we have them, for they are an important source of new ideas and provide a critical dimension to intra-party debate. But these individuals, like their aberrant Democratic counterparts, do not represent the dominant trend of the GOP, which is more conservative.

What is conservatism? To me, a conservative is one who believes that government should only do for people that which they need done but cannot accomplish on their own. He possesses a strong belief in the power of the individual citizen to ascertain his own needs and determine the best way to take care of them. He places a premium on maximum governmental efficiency with minimum governmental interference.

To be a Republican is to reject the simplistic notion that money alone is the answer to every problem. Just as important, and often times more important, is the manner in which the money is spent. Republicans recognize the value of restraint, the merit in moderation. We feel strongly that there are some things that the federal government cannot do and shouldn't even try to do.

Our philosophy is best manifested in programs such as federal revenue sharing. That is the program that each year returns a portion of federally-collected tax dollars to the states for them to allocate according to their own priorities. Revenue sharing personifies the Republican approach to government. Yet it is an anathema to most Democrats. A report published by a subcommittee of the House Government Operations Committee revealed that many Democrats in the 93rd Congress opposed the concept of revenue sharing. Therefore it is not surprising that the program's future is in serious trouble (in spite of the fact that the program has the enthusiastic support of the bipartisan Conference of U.S. Mayors).

Warned *Washington Post* columnist David Broder in May of 1974: "If the Democrats are greatly augmented in numbers in the November election, a major push to terminate general revenue sharing or to tie it more tightly to federal priority programs may be expected in the next Congress." When the voters gave the Democrats a two-to-one majority in the 94th Congress, I wonder if they fully realized the possible consequences of their vote with regard to such programs as revenue sharing?

What about the prospects for getting the Republican message across to the people of the country? Recent events would suggest that our chances, if properly utilized, are good. There was a time not long ago when the moderate Republican philosophy of state and local control was mainly unwelcome and out of place.

But times change and now, given a budget deficit of more than $74 billion and a federal bureaucracy considerably larger than it was 20 years ago, Republicans aren't looking so bad. "Republicans speak this language [the language of small government] far more fluently than Democrats," conceded *News-*

week Magazine, "and it is the GOP that has come closest to a programmatic approach to the new politics."

Republicans are looking better to the American people because our proposals make good sense for the 1970s. We are also looking better because of the mental sterility of the Democratic Party. Think about it: Can you name any new idea that congressional Democrats have had in the last 30 years? I certainly cannot. On the critical energy problem, the Democrats opposed our decontrol program but failed to come up with anything new of their own. On the equally critical problem of unemployment, their only answer has been to bring out the old 1930s public works programs which did nothing to solve unemployment then and would only make the economy worse now.

The same thing cannot be said of the Republican Party. Mainly through our efforts, the nation has a highly popular and effective program of revenue sharing. We have developed brand new programs aimed at creating jobs, encouraging energy production and supplementing social security. We have developed a long list of specific reforms for the legislative process. We have been innovative; the Democratic Party has not.

If ever there was a time for a resurgence in Republican Party strength, that time is now. Coincidentally, our time of greatest opportunity is also our time of greatest danger. For if we fail to seize the initiative and capitalize on the deficiencies of the Democrats in Congress, then our death notice will have been signed. If the GOP does not experience a significant change in political fortunes by 1978, it is likely that we will go the way of the Whigs.

Congress and the two-party system in America deserve a better fate. The chance for a new Congress under Republican control in 1977 is a realistic possibility and we do not even have to pick up all of the 74 House seats needed to attain the numerical majority of 218.

Just before the start of the 95th Congress, a number of conservative House Democrats may decide to switch their party allegiance and elect a Republican Speaker of the House.

There has always been pre-session talk about the fact that many conservative Democrats are disgruntled with the leftward direction of their party. Since they consistently vote with Republicans, they may just want to make it official and become Republicans themselves.

Up to now, it has been only talk. But there is reason to believe that next year may be different. Why? Because of the ever-increasing unpredictability of the liberal Democratic Caucus.

At the start of the 94th Congress, the Caucus succeeded in ousting three committee chairmen, mainly for ideological reasons: the late Congressman Wright Patman of Banking, Currency, and Housing, William Poage of Agriculture and F. Edward Herbert of Armed Services. The removal of the three chairmen has made many conservative Democrats nervous. In years past, their only real reason for remaining in a party whose mainstream was not to their liking was the considerable seniority they had accrued. Now, however, they have no assurance that their seniority will save them. Phillip Burton's liberal Caucus is not exactly the safest place for a conservative Democrat to reside. Many may decide it is better to jump off a sinking ship than be pushed off later.

I am realistic about this. I know full well that conservative Democrats are not going to cross the aisle in order to make a larger minority. They will only come across if by doing so they will succeed in making a new majority . . . a Republican majority.

That means that Republicans must pick up enough House seats on their own to make a conservative Democratic defection a genuine possibility. Realizing that it takes 218 Members to make a majority, I believe we must reach somewhere in

the neighborhood of 200 by ourselves. If we can pick up 56 seats in November, there may be a group of conservative Democrats who will be giving serious thought to changing their party affiliation. If they become convinced that collectively they can create a new majority, there is a strong probability that they will make their move. The key factor in this entire equation, however, is a Republican win of 56 new House seats.

Republicans will need the help of certain Democrats to gain control of the House, just as we have needed their help to successfully block so many bad pieces of legislation advanced by the majority. By obtaining Democratic support, we have been able to sustain presidential vetoes of misdirected bills with remarkable constancy in spite of our small numbers.

The so-called jobs bill is one good case in point. There once was a time when a Member of Congress dared not vote against any bill with the word jobs in the title, particularly during a period of high unemployment. But the Emergency Employment Appropriations bill passed by the Democratic Congress in May of 1975 was too bad to be believed. This $5.3 billion monstrosity contained such dubious items as the purchase of 21,000 automobiles for federal agencies, a provision that proponents of the bill meekly explained was aimed at stimulating the lagging auto industry. Most of the jobs to be created by the bill were of the public sector variety—the usual Democratic leaf-raking approach to unemployment. To make matters worse, the great bulk of the jobs would not materialize until at least 1977!

So bad was the Democratic jobs bill that virtually every major newspaper from the *Washington Star* to *The New York Times* to the *Wall Street Journal* editorialized against it.

President Ford wisely vetoed it. Then it was up to the Republican minority to block the two-thirds majority needed to override his veto. We did so by sticking together in the national interest. Our own cohesiveness, coupled with the votes of conservative Democrats who also recognized the serious deficiencies of the jobs bill, spared the nation a non-remedy for a real problem.

Immediately following our victory on the Floor, we offered a substitute emergency employment bill with a price tag less than half that of the Democratic version. We also offered a separate bill to provide almost half a million dollars for summer jobs for young people. The Democrats, having been soundly beaten on their programs, reluctantly accepted our substitutes. Both were passed and signed into law by President Ford.

The jobs bill is but one example of how the small Republican minority, working together with like-minded conservative Democrats, have scored important victories in the national interest. There have been many others. President Ford found it necessary to veto a total of 17 bills in 1975. Thanks to our small but mighty minority, the Democrats were able to override the President only three times.

If I sound boastful it's because I am. At the start of the 94th Congress, in which the Democrats outnumbered Republicans two-to-one, I predicted that the tiny GOP minority would turn out to be the largest cohesive force in Washington. My prediction definitely came to pass. On key vote after key vote, from jobs to agriculture to strip mining, congressional Republicans made a big difference. By sticking together when it counted, we were able to force the other side to go beyond the usual slogans and rhetoric and accept some sensible programs.

My point is this: If congressional Republicans can produce important results in a minority condition—particularly in a badly reduced minority condition—imagine what we can produce as a majority, with the votes to enact a program of our own. Imagine what we can accomplish working with a completely revamped legislative process, with brand new jurisdictional lines between committees, smoother procedures and better rules. With our demonstrated ability to stay together, and working in a new system that responds to leadership initiative, Republicans can snap Congress right out of its disgraceful lethargy and begin to get some results for the country.

All we need is 218 warm Republican bodies in the House and 51 in the Senate, and we will give America a Congress that gets things done. That would be a new experience for the people of the country, an experience that they have sorely missed, and badly need.

It can happen. It will happen. I believe that it must happen.

NOTES

1. "The House is Troubled", WASHINGTON POST, (June 22, 1975).

2. Warren Weaver, Jr., *BOTH YOUR HOUSES,* (Washington, D.C. Praeger Publications, 1972) p. 83.

3. CONGRESSIONAL RECORD, (July 31, 1975) p. H 8022.

4. Former Rep. H. Allen Smith (R-Calif.), Ranking Republican Representative on Rules Committee, in a letter to the *Congress Project,* July 25, 1972.

5. CONGRESSIONAL RECORD, (July 31, 1975) p. H 8018.

6. Lindley H. Clark, Jr., WALL STREET JOURNAL, (August 18, 1975).

7. Irving Kristol, WALL STREET JOURNAL, (Nov. 17, 1974).

8. Stephen E. Nordlinger, "Politics Decided House Energy Debate," BALTIMORE SUN, (August 1, 1975).

121

9. CONGRESSIONAL QUARTERLY, (August 9, 1975) p. 1802.

10. Ralph K. Huitt (and Robert L. Peabody), *CONGRESS: TWO DECADES OF ANALYSIS* (Harper and Row, 1969), p. 144.

11. Donald Lambro, POWER ON THE POTOMAC: "The Federal Rathole: 50 Easy Ways To Plug It.", WASHINGTONIAN MAGAZINE, (August, 1975) p. 165.

12. In Debate: Senator John F. Kennedy and Vice President Richard Nixon First Joint Radio-Television Broadcast
Monday, September 26, 1960
Originating CBS, Chicago, Illinois (Broadcast on all Networks)

13. Remarks of Senator John F. Kennedy, Street Rally, Phoenix, Arizona (November 3, 1960).

Appendix

I: REPUBLICANS VS. DEMOCRATS IN THE 94TH CONGRESS: THE ECONOMY

Congressional Record: June 5, 1975

MAJORITY LEADER THOMAS P. O'NEILL, JR., SAYS, THE VOTE AGAINST JOBS IS A VOTE AGAINST THE PEOPLE

(Mr. O'NEILL asked and was given permission to address the House for 1 minute, to revise and extend his remarks and include extraneous matter.)

Mr. O'NEILL. Mr. Speaker, President Ford is making his economic program very clear: no to the farmers—no to the unemployed—no to everybody from youth to the elderly.

The White House went all out yesterday to beat the override on the emergency jobs bill. They pulled out all the stops. But it was a clear test of the differences between the two parties in this Congress. The result was that 92% of the Democrats voted for jobs and 87% of the Republicans voted against jobs.

What the Republicans won was a vote against the people. It was a vote for recession.

What it means is more suffering for those who have already suffered most, more billions for unemployment benefits, more welfare, more

123

incentive for crime, more of all the other ills that go along with outrageous unemployment.

President Ford can make all the rosy predictions he wants about economic recovery next year. The fact is that unemployment shot up 65% since he took office 10 months ago. The rate is going to top nine percent when the new figures come out tomorrow.

Nine million people are out of work, and all the administration does is announce that things might get better sometime. Maybe that is all President Ford can offer to the people of this country, but Congress has got to do a lot better than that.

We Democrats in this Congress have got to stand up for the people.

A DEPRESSION, NOT A RECESSION

(Mr. HAYS of Ohio asked and was given permission to address the House for 1 minute, and to revise and extend his remarks.)

Mr. HAYS of Ohio. Mr. Speaker, I think the speech of the majority leader, the gentleman from Massachusetts (Mr. O'NEILL), hit right on target. I would just like to add an observation of my own. I keep reading these reports in the press from Secretary Simon, Mr. Zarb, the energy czar, and other Cabinet officers, about the recession has bottomed out, and things are going to pick up, and so on. I have to believe that they are doing a scissors and paste job from the newspapers of the era of 1929 through 1932 because in those days every time you picked up a paper some Cabinet officer was saying that things were going to get better, but the Republican administration at that time was doing things to make things worse.

The veto of the jobs bill is a good example. If we had 1 million more people working we would have two million more people paying taxes, because those extra million people working would create another million jobs in private industry. But, no, the vicious circle goes on, while at the same time you read the statements that these nincompoops put out about the recession has bottomed out, and in the same paper on the same page you read a story about another industry laying off 20,000 people, another industry laying off 50,000 people, another industry closing down for five weeks, and so on.

If there is going to be any relief for the American people from this depression—not a recession, but a depression—it is going to have to come from the Democratic Party and from the Democrats in the Congress.

THE CORRECTNESS OF THE ADMINISTRATION'S POLICY

(Mr. RHODES asked and was given permission to address the House for 1 minute, and to revise and extend his remarks.)

Mr. RHODES. Mr. Speaker, It has been with great interest that I have listened to the speech of the distinguished majority leader, the gentleman from Massachusetts (Mr. O'NEILL), and that of the gentleman from Ohio (Mr. HAYS).

The gentleman from Ohio mentioned 1929 through 1932 as the time when there was a depression. I hasten to remind the gentleman that the depression did not end in 1932 when the Democratic Party assumed power. In fact, it was still very much going on some six years later when rearmament for World War II began. In 1940, 14.6% of the civilian labor force was out of work. It was not until the following year—the first year of the Second World War—that unemployment dropped to 9.9%. So the record of the Democratic Party in curing depressions is not a very good one.

Insofar as the situation now is concerned, the Democrats have adopted a worm's eye view in looking at our economy. They are so busy looking at that hillock up ahead that they cannot see beyond what is there. They expect us to do the same thing.

I serve notice on them that we are not going to do that. Republicans are not going to look at the economy as the Democrats think it is, or as they might wish it is. We are going to look at the economy as it is and will be.

I think that the economic policies of the administration are sound. The administration has the only program in town for getting us out of the recession and at the same time to protect the economy from the ravages of inflation.

The main trouble with the reasoning of the Members on the other side of the aisle is that they have come to the conclusion that expenditure in the public sector is the do-all and the end-all, and it is not. We Republicans still believe we need to provide jobs for people in our factories, but not just public jobs. There must be more than jobs raking leaves. That is the chief difference between these two parties.

II: REPUBLICANS VS. DEMOCRATS IN THE 94TH CONGRESS: JOBS

Congressional Record: June 10, 1975

CONGRESS WILL NOT ACCEPT REPUBLICAN FULL UNEMPLOYMENT POLICY

(Mr. O'NEILL asked and was given permission to address the House for 1 minute and to revise and extend his remarks.)

Mr. O'Neill. Mr. Speaker, I regret the fact that the leadership on the other side of the aisle is not here to hear what I have to say.

President Ford said in his press conference last night: that he still cannot decide————.

Mr. RHODES. Mr. Speaker, will the gentleman yield?

Mr. O'NEILL. I yield to the distinguished minority leader.

Mr. RHODES. Mr. Speaker, I just want to announce my presence.

Mr. O'NEILL. All right. Mr. Speaker, I shall address my remarks particularly, of course, to the minority leader.

Mr. Speaker, President Ford said last night in his press conference he still cannot decide when to announce his candidacy for 1976.

I hope he is not waiting for better news on the jobs front. The unemployment figures for May were even worse than I had expected. I really did not believe he could mess up the economy as badly as he has. Not only did unemployment exceed 9 percent, but it went up to 9.2 percent. As a result, there are now 8½ million Americans out of work, up 360,000 last month—the worst job picture since 1940. On top of that, four million students are out of school this month and looking for summer jobs.

So President Ford has vetoed a bill that would have created 900,000 direct full-time jobs and taken care of 20% of the summer jobs. We do not know how many extra jobs that would have meant in the private sector.

He accused Congress of being fiscally irresponsible in creating these jobs. That is a lot better than being socially irresponsible and doing nothing about unemployment. All the business signs and statistics and Republican wishful thinking in the world will not put people back to work.

It takes jobs to do that. President Ford told the press that there does not have to be any more confrontation with the Congress, providing that the Congress does what he says.

Congress does not work for the President. The Congress works for the people. This Congress is not about to accept any Republican economic policy of full unemployment. We continue our work on the job bills for the people and for the economy, and we will send to the Members many more pieces of legislation, hoping that we can stimulate this economy.

PRESIDENT FORD WILL RUN FOR REELECTION

(Mr. RHODES asked and was given permission to address the House for 1 minute and to revise and extend his remarks.)

Mr. RHODES. Mr. Speaker, it was a pleasure for me to be on the floor at the time that my delightful friend, the majority leader, the gentleman from Massachusetts (Mr. O'NEILL), was asking questions about the future of the President of the United States.

I can assure my good friend that the President of the United States, in due time, will announce his candidacy for reelection. At the risk of offending my good friend, the gentleman from Arizona (Mr. UDALL), who is a candidate for the Presidency, let me announce that I will begin to take bets at that time, that the present President of the United States will be elected.

The gentleman from Massachusetts (Mr. O'NEILL) has at some length deplored the fact that the President of the United States refused to buy him a year's supply of Band-Aids for the economy in the shape of the leaf-raking jobs bill. The facts are that the economy is in recession and inflation mainly because of the fact that the Democratic Congresses through the years have operated at deficits and caused the inflationary spiral to go right through the roof. That is the reason that we have unemployment. What the gentleman wants to do is to compound the felony by spending more through the public sector, causing more inflation. Apparently he thinks that in some magical way this will cure unemployment in the country. Of course it will not.

Mr. Speaker, all that the Democratic leadership is doing is again adopting the methods which did not work in the 1930s. The gentleman says that unemployment of 9.2% is bad, and it is; but it is not as bad as the 9.9% unemployment which we still had when World War II began, after seven years of the Roosevelt administration, which spent and spent.

Mr. Speaker, I invite the Democratic side to cooperate with the minority in finding some means of helping the private enterprise economy of this country. Mainly, this would be by doing those things necessary to get the Federal Government out of the position of impeding our economic progress.

III: REPUBLICANS VS. DEMOCRATS IN THE 94TH CONGRESS: VETOES

Congressional Record: June 20, 1975

MAJORITY LEADER THOMAS P. O'NEILL, JR., SAYS PRESIDENT IS BUILDING A PLATFORM OUT OF VETOES

(Mr. O'NEILL asked and was given permission to address the House for 1 minute and to revise and extend his remarks.)

Mr. O'NEILL. Mr. Speaker, I regret to see that the minority leader is not here this morning. I presume he is busy writing letters to the editor. I want to give him something he can put in a letter to the editor.

Mr. Speaker, President Ford has let it be known that he is going to veto two more bills, including one that Congress has not even passed yet. This is the consumer protection bill.

The other new veto will be the middle-income housing bill, which also provides mortgage help to homeowners who are out of a job.

This is what I call thinking ahead negatively. In the housing industry, things have been so bad for so long that last month's housing starts—which were low for May—came out looking like a big improvement in comparison. The fact is that unemployment in the construction industry is still 22%. The administration is not going to do anything about it, except veto a housing bill.

The President's six strategic vetoes so far this year have already had more adverse effects on our people than all 23 of his successful vetoes in the last Congress put together. If he keeps on at this rate, he is going to set a new record for the Republican administration.

President Ford is trying to build a platform of vetoes. In my opinion, we are only really dubbing him "King Veto." He is running on a full employment policy. When he makes predictions about a rosy turnaround in the economy, he is talking about from a big business, big money point of view. What he is giving the people is a rosy runaround.

ANSWER TO CHARGES OF CONGRESSIONAL INACTION

Mr. RHODES. Mr. Chairman, this morning, when the House went into session, the majority leader, the distinguished gentleman from Massachusetts (Mr. O'NEILL) took the floor, as he has frequently done in recent days, to present his usual diatribe on the subject of congressional inaction and Presidential veto.

The majority leader made a special point, as he has done several times, of the fact that I was not present to hear his remarks. I believe I owe him an explanation. I wish he were here. I note that he did not vote on the last amendment, so I assume he has left Washington for his home, and I wish him a happy weekend.

At the time the majority leader was presenting his partisan views, I was concluding a meeting at my office with the new chairman of the Governors' Conference, the Honorable Robert Ray of Iowa. Governor Ray is in town to meet with congressional leaders, as well as the President, to discuss some of the problems facing the States.

And I might say that I have had that appointment for quite some time. I did not realize the House would be meeting at 10 o'clock, otherwise I might have changed the appointment. But since I had the appointment, I thought I should keep it. With all due respect to the gentleman from Massachusetts, my judgment was that it was more important for me to hear Governor Ray's analysis of State problems than it was for me to be present to hear the majority leader's partisan discourse, which is becoming increasingly predictable. In fact, I believe I could give each one of them for him.

I would also like to say to the majority leader, as well as to all my friends on the majority side of the aisle, that while I am proud that by sticking together the Republican minority and the President have been able to spare the Nation some truly bad legislation, I have been saying all along that Government by veto is no way to run the country. The House Republican leadership has been calling on the majority to agree to join with us in a "consensus" arrangement. We have said that the American people do not deserve stalemate. They did not vote for stalemate. They expect Congress to act.

We have expressed our willingness to work with the majority on legislation to enact at once these things upon which we have agreed and put aside for the moment areas of disagreement. In response, all we get is partisan rhetoric from the other side.

I would like to make a suggestion. When the majority leader determines that he has something positive to say, when he desires to address himself and his party to the importance of ending the stalemate and getting something done, I hope he will inform me. I assure him that I will make it a special point to be here to listen. If I am not on the floor he can call me. If he does not know my extension number, it is 50600, and whenever he calls me and asks me to be present on the floor because he has something to say, I assure him I will be here.

IV: REPUBLICANS VS. DEMOCRATS IN THE 94TH CONGRESS: GOP LEGISLATIVE AGENDA

Congressional Record: September 10, 1975

MAJORITY LEADER THOMAS P. O'NEILL, JR., SAYS REPUBLICAN PROGRAM IS THE BEST REASON FOR CONTINUED DEMOCRATIC CONTROL OF CONGRESS

(Mr. O'NEILL asked and was given permission to address the House for one minute and to revise and extend his remarks.)

Mr. O'NEILL. Mr. Speaker, the Republican legislative program announced by the distinguished minority leader is the best reason I can think of for continued control of the Congress by the Democratic Party—which is the party of the people and not of big business and special interests.

There is not a single new idea in this package. In some instances, it follows the well-worn Republican pattern of picking up a Democratic innovation about 20 years later and announcing that it is something new.

I must say that this program is replete with all the Republican platitudes that I have ever heard in my entire career in public service. This program stands for the protection of big business and their interpretation of the free enterprise system.

President Ford and the Republicans in the House have this much in common—they can never seem to catch up with the needs and wants of the American people.

This program appears to be the work of an ad hoc committee appointed by the minority leader of former Congressmen who were all defeated in the last election.

This program is consistent in one respect. I see where the Republicans have chosen Kansas City for their convention next year. The last time they were there they chose Herbert Hoover. He would be comfortable with this program. The Grand Old Party, the Republican Party, has not changed since.

REPLY TO THE MAJORITY LEADER ON THE REPUBLICAN LEGISLATIVE AGENDA

(Mr. RHODES asked and was given permission to address the House for one minute and to revise and extend his remarks.)

Mr. RHODES. Mr. Speaker, I was amused at the remarks of my genial friend, the majority leader. I gathered from the remarks that the majority leader does not exactly approve of the Republican legislative program. In many ways I think this is probably the best portent of success that the program has had yet. I did not expect the gentleman to approve it. I would have been disappointed if he had.

As a matter of fact, there is much that is innovative. The fact that it calls for a balanced budget in three years is certainly innovative, because the Democrats have controlled the Congress for the last 40 years, with a few years' exceptions.

Mr. O'NEILL. Mr. Speaker, will the gentleman yield?

Mr. RHODES. I do not yield now.

The fact that the gentleman from Massachusetts also saw fit to call attention to the fact that the Republican Convention will be held in Kansas City causes me to reflect on several points. One of them is that as far as I know Kansas City is not a bankrupt city, but is one of our more progressive municipalities.

As far as convention sites go, it is perhaps appropriate that the party that ran New York into the hole should meet there amid the governmental ruins of their operation. The city's dilemma is illustrated by the fact that the Statue of Liberty is now holding a tin cup. The Democrats should feel right at home. They have run Uncle Sam a half trillion in hock, and they have made New York into sad city. Perhaps, in all honesty, since the purveyor's of fiscal irresponsibilities will be gathering there—they should really call this the Debt-ocratic Convention.

My hope is that we will adopt the Republican legislative agenda so that the sad plight of New York City does not become the fate of our Nation.

V: THE HOUSE REPUBLICAN TASK FORCE ON REFORM, FIRST REPORT, 94TH CONGRESS: "THE STRUGGLE FOR COMPREHENSIVE REFORM IS JUST BEGINNING."

Congressional Record: March 10, 1975

Bill Frenzel, Chairman, Edward G. Biester, Caldwell Butler, Del Clawson, Jim Cleveland, Thad Cochran, Barber Conable, Millicent Fenwick, Lou Frey, Jr., Trent Lott, W. Henson Moore, Joel Pritchard, Ralph Regula, Virginia Smith, Bill Steiger, Charles Wiggins. Ex officio Members: John B. Anderson, John Rhodes.
House Republican Research Committee, March 1975.

FINDINGS AND RECOMMENDATIONS

Despite ongoing attempts at reform by concerned Members of both parties, the House of Representatives does not function well. It rates low marks in effectiveness, in representativeness and in public confidence.

Its rules are antiquated, its customs secretive, and its procedures often in conflict with democratic principles. The American people have little confidence in it.

The House Republican Task Force on Reform is not satisfied with the modest successes of the status quo. We are determined to make the House as effective as representative and as respectable as possible.

Reform means more than change. It means improvement. Comprehensive congressional reform cannot be accomplished by a few changes in caucus procedures or by juggling a few chairmen. Real reform transcends personalities and party politics. It requires sweeping changes that will have an enduring impact on the House.

We urge House Members of both parties to rise to the challenge of reform, to join us in implementing our proposals, to explore other changes, and to make reform an urgent priority of this Congress.

We especially invite the majority party to join us. We note that, despite its proclaimed commitment to reform, the record of the Democratic Caucus in this Congress has been anti-reform. Particularly disappointing have been the repeated instances of backtracking on positive changes previously adopted by the House. At a time when the House should be marching forward on reform, we regret that nearly half of our recommendations must deal with cleaning up backward anti-reform steps adopted this session by the majority.

Specifically, these retrogressions include binding by caucus, reinstatement of proxy voting, increased use of the suspension calendar. staff stealing, more closed rules and secret caucus meetings.

The Task Force believes the struggle for comprehensive reform is just beginning. It has selected 16 areas where significant improvements can be made now. Our list is not complete. Much more is required, and the Task Force hopes to continue with further recommendations.

But this list represents well-known and well-debated changes which can be implemented if the House has the will:

1. Open rules; fewer waivers of points of order.
2. Open committee meetings; open conference committees.
3. Open committee records; recorded votes.
4. Improved lobby disclosure.
5. Better Congressional oversight.
6. Revised Committee jurisdiction.
7. Broadcast of floor proceedings.
8. Reduced and controlled suspensions of rules.
9. Better scheduling of House business.
10. Realistic and accurate Congressional Record.
11. Control and disclosure of newsletter funds.
12. No "unit rule" caucus votes.
13. One-third minority staffing.
14. No proxy voting.
15. Fair apportionment on committees.
16. No weakening of quorum rules.

OPEN RULES, POINTS OF ORDER AND NONGERMANE SENATE AMENDMENTS

The Task Force vigorously supports full and free debate and deliberation in the House of Representatives. We make the following recommendations to provide the most free and open environment for all House deliberations:

1. Open Rules. *All legislation should be considered under an open rule.* The Task Force is disturbed by the frequency with which the closed rule has been employed early in this Congress. While committees generally do a very competent job, all legislation should be the product of all of the people's representatives, not just a select few. In the future, the Democratic leadership should seek to curb the tendency to avoid controversial, important issues by putting legislation up on the Floor under a closed rule. Open rules are another method of bringing sunshine into the legislative process.

There are occasions when an open rule should be conditioned. It is not sufficient, however, to open up legislation only to those few key amendments blessed by the majority caucus. The only conditions open rules should carry are requirements that amendments be considered by the appropriate legislative committee and that amendments be printed in the Record prior to consideration on the Floor.

An additional problem arises when the Democratic caucus binds its Members to vote for a closed rule. Elsewhere, we have recommended that this practice be prohibited. At minimum, when such a vote is taken in caucus, the complete record of the proceedings and the results of the vote (including the way each Member voted) should be made public.

2. Points of order. The same general principles apply to waiving points of order. This procedure is used far too frequently and broadly. *The power to grant waivers should be used only in extreme emergencies and, when granted, should be very specific.* Blanket waivers are not conducive to the production of sound legislation.

3. Nongermane amendments. Senate rules allow amendments to legislation that are not relevant to the matter under consideration, while House rules forbid their consideration except when points of order are waived. Even then, the House may demand a separate recorded vote on any nongermane senate amendment. These Senate amendments, which often have not been seen, studied or discussed by House Members, are accepted without hearings, mark up or debate in committee and without amendment or debate on the floor. *Since they represent a suspension of House Rules, a two-thirds vote should be required for adoption instead of a simple majority.*

OPEN MEETINGS

The Task Force strongly believes that all of the public's business should be conducted in the open, except when the interest of the public itself dictates otherwise. Public confidence in the legislative process is ill-served by meetings shrouded in secrecy and closed to public scrutiny. The compelling policy considerations requiring openness apply with equal force to party meetings which decide public questions. The Task Force condemns the rule of the Democratic Caucus which tolerates secret votes on important public issues and compounds the error by binding all of the Democratic members to vote in future public meetings in accordance with the will of the majority of their members expressed in private.

In furtherance of sound public policy for the conduct of all meetings, the Task Force recommends:

1. *All Committee sessions, including subcommittees, joint and select committees and conference, should be open to the public,* except in those instances where a full discussion of the issues before the Committee might:

(a) Tend to degrade, defame or ridicule any person;

(b) Unreasonably invade the private or personal affairs of any person;

(c) Reveal private proprietary information of any business entity; or

(d) Reveal information inimical to important National interests.

2. A record vote to close a Committee session should be required in each instance where it is necessary to protect the interests stated above, and no session should remain closed for any period longer than is necessary to do so.

3. *Conference Committees should be open unless voted closed, per No. two above, by a majority of the House managers and by a majority of the Senate managers.*

4. Congressional Party Caucuses and Conferences should be open whenever votes are taken which bind Members of Congress or decide public questions.

The Task Force supports several additional proposals to the Rules of the House designed to further open committee deliberations to the public and make committees more accountable to the people.

The first proposal would make the complete record of committee action available for public inspection, except for such material the committee determines would either endanger National security or violate any law or rule of the House. While the present House rule requires that such a complete record shall be kept, only the roll call votes are open to the public. It is important that the people not only know how their representatives vote in committee, but the full context in which such decisions are made, including individual positions taken and arguments made prior to each vote. This is particularly important since many key decisions are made by non-record, voice or division votes (which are not now part of the public record). While it may seem superfluous to open to the public the complete record of committee action since we have already recommended that committee meetings be open, it should be recognized that most meetings draw few spectators and often no media representatives. It is, therefore, in the public interest that the written record be open for subsequent inspection by interested parties.

The second proposal provides that any member of a committee may demand a roll call vote on any question. During the last Congress, some committees provided that either one-fifth of those present or one-fifth of a quorum was needed to demand a roll call (the former practice is actually in violation of the House rules).

Thirdly, recorded votes should be required on any bill or resolution reported from a Committee. We strongly feel that the people have a right to know how their representatives vote in committee, and that recorded votes should be easily obtained and frequently demanded.

136

We believe that organized lobbying activities should be fully disclosed so that the people may know the influences at work in the operation of their Government. We do not believe, however, that regulation of such activities should prevent or restrict people from petitioning their Government.

The Federal Regulation of Lobbying Act, passed in 1946, was Congress's initial effort to allow greater public scrutiny of the lobbying process. Lacking an effective enforcement mechanism and weakened by a Supreme Court decision, the Act has been termed more loophole than law.

In 1974, five states passed new laws or regulations for lobby disclosure—Arizona, California, Kansas, Minnesota, and West Virginia. Of the states with lobby disclosure or regulation statutes, over half of them impose standards and requirements stricter than the Federal statute.

The states are moving—and so should the Congress. We specifically urge the Congress to strengthen existing lobby disclosure requirements as follows:

1. During its 28-year lifespan, the present law produced only one successful prosecution, and that occurred only after the defendant agreed to plead guilty. The Act does not provide for the monitoring of, compliance with, and enforcement of its own provisions. We recommend that the *administration and enforcement of the law be placed in the Federal Election Commission, with both subpoena and civil enforcement powers*. Criminal prosecutions should remain in the Justice Department.

2. We recommend that the Commission be empowered to make audits and field investigations, to subpoena records on information exempted from disclosure and to compile and publicize information of value to the general public in scrutinizing lobbying activities.

3. A major loophole in the current law is its criteria for identifying lobbyists. Many lobbying groups presently do not register because of a 1954 Supreme Court rule requiring registration only by organizations whose "principal purpose" is lobbying. *We recommend that disclosure requirements be based on an expenditure threshold*. Recognizing the need for a *de minimis* concept to facilitate administration and to meet constitutional requirements, we recommend that this threshold be set at a reasonable, specific dollar figure, perhaps around $1000 per quarter.

4. We recommend that lobby disclosure regulations NOT include the following types of activities: (a) an appearance before a congressional committee or the submission of a written statement to any Federal executive department, agency or entity; (2) any communication or solicitation through the distribution in the normal course of business of any news, editorial view, letter to the editor advertising or

similar matter by newspapers, magazines, publishers or radio and TV broadcasters.

5. The Task Force is greatly concerned that burdensome registration and reporting requirements will have a chilling effect on public debate and the right of citizens to petition their government. Accordingly, we recommend that the lobbying law impose no unreasonable burdens on individuals lobbying independently on their own individual behalf. Specifically, travel expenses, mailing costs and other similar items should be exempted and not credited toward the dollar threshold. The Commission should have the power and authority to supervise these exceptions to see that they are not abused. We fear that any blanket overly-broad statute not containing exemptions similar to the above will abridge precious citizens' rights and will be struck down by the courts.

6. We recommend that persons who must register as lobbyists be required to maintain records *which identify the source of any income or contribution in excess of $100 used for lobbying purposes and identify each expenditure (not exempted in recommendation four & five) over $100 made in the course of lobbying.*

7. We recommend retention of the current requirement that lobbyists report their specific categories of legislative interest.

8. The current law requires the reporting of lobbying activities within the legislative branch and totally ignores such activities within the Executive Branch. *We recommend that lobbying activities within the Executive Branch be subject to similar disclosure requirements.*

9. Public interest groups have urged that executive agencies and Members of Congress be required to log contacts made by lobbyists, as Federal Energy Administration officials now do. Such a logging system may be helpful if it applies exclusively to formal communications between lobbyists and congressional committees, independent commissions and departments of government. We believe, however, that such a scheme would be unreasonable for the many daily contacts between Members of Congress and their constituents and for informal contacts between lobbyists and bureaucrats. It would place a burdensome requirement on government officials. It would tend to limit accessibility of officials at a time when we are urging openness. *We specifically recommend that, except as noted above, a mandatory scheme of logging all contacts and communications not be adopted.*

CONGRESSIONAL OVERSIGHT OF FEDERAL PROGRAMS

Congressional oversight was formally initiated by the Legislative Reorganization Act of 1946 which required each standing committee of the Congress to exercise continuous watchfulness of all Federal programs under its jurisdiction.

The failure of the Congress to conduct periodic review of Federal programs caused Congress itself to make this mandate more explicit in the Legislative Reorganization Act of 1970, by requiring each standing committee of the House to conduct reviews and studies on a continuing basis.

The Intergovernmental Cooperation Act of 1968 required each congressional committee to conduct oversight and review of open-ended State-Fed. grant-in-aid programs every fourth year. Congressional compliance with this mandate of law has been almost nonexistent.

The 1974 report of the Select Committee on Committees made extensive recommendations for overhauling Congressional oversight of Federal programs but the plan was watered down, due to opposition by House Democrats.

We believe that adequate congressional oversight is needed to reveal the flaws and inefficiencies of Federal programs and to point towards more effective alternatives. Because Congress has not exercised its oversight responsibilities, some government programs have become duplicative, wasteful, mismanaged, or otherwise not cost effective. Others have become inoperative.

Today, three-fourths of all Federal expenditures are mandated. Without critical analysis of and changes in existing programs, there will be no funds available for new initiatives and proposals needed to solve urgent National problems.

The Task Force believes that the Congress' failure to conduct adequate oversight has had deleterious effects on the economic health and well-being of our society, and that better oversight can help save taxpayers' dollars and improve program administration.

RECOMMENDATIONS

To improve the quality of Congressional oversight, the Task Force:

1. *Urges the Government Operations Committee to monitor strictly the oversight activities of House Committees* and call attention to the oversight failings of the Congress. Only through careful oversight hearings can congressional and public attention be focused on government agencies and programs which should either be altered, replaced, or abolished.

2. Proposes that at the beginning of each Congress *all standing committees make a report to the Government Operations Committee on their plans for oversight,* including agendas of oversight activities and timetables for completion of those agendas. The Government Operations Committee shall make these reports public and may standardize them and specify items to be included in the initial report, as well as in the final report presently required at the end of each Congress by existing House rules.

3. Recommends *full compliance with the Intergovernmental Cooperation Act of 1968* which require thorough review of all open-ended,

Federal grant-in-aid programs every four years and urges that the Act be extended to include all federal grant-in-aid programs and tax subsidies. To insure compliance, we recommend that every program not reviewed every four years shall be terminated automatically.

4. Endorses the provision of the Select Committee on Committee's report which would allow the Committee on Government Operations to offer Committee amendments based on review and oversight findings that have been included as part of the committee report.

5. Urges each committee to make its first priority the review and oversight of Federal programs. Critical analysis of existing programs is a more urgent need than the initiation of new frequently overlapping and conflicting Federal legislation. Special attention should be given to bureaucratic red tape and to regulations which, in the name of carrying out the intent of the law, place needless burdens on the American people.

REFORMING COMMITTEE JURISDICTION

The failure of the 93rd Congress to adopt substantive reform in the area of jurisdiction of House committees is a singular failure.

We believe that the concepts contained in the report of the Select Committee on Committees deserve consideration and action by the 94th Congress. We are willing to assist the majority in having the Committee on Rules undertake the necessary work to complete action on the whole area of jurisdictional reform.

We believe that the 94th Congress should:

1. Provide for a committee system in which each member serves on but one major committee which has substantive responsibility;

2. Reshape the present incredible hodgepodge of conflicting jurisdictions;

3. Distribute the workload of House committees more logically and equitably.

When the 93rd Congress debated and voted on the work of the Select Committee on Committees, the vast majority of Republicans were willing to take on the power structure of the House of Representatives. One of the great disappointments was the overwhelming failure of Democrats to face up to their responsibility in helping to reshape the House of Representatives so that it would be a more responsive and responsible institution.

BROADCASTING OF HOUSE FLOOR PROCEEDINGS

As "the people's branch," Congress has a special obligation to open its activities and proceedings to the widest possible public view.

Accordingly, *the Task Force proposes that the House authorize complete, live radio and television coverage of its floor proceedings,* to be initiated—as recommended by the Joint Committee on Con-

gressional Operations—on the basis of a one-year pilot program.
There are compelling reasons for authorizing the broadcasting of floor sessions:

1. The sharply declining regard in which the public holds its Congress can be attributed, in part at least, to a lack of understanding of the role, functions, and procedures of the Congress—a condition which Congress can help correct by opening the legislative process to greater public scrutiny.

2. The Executive Branch's extensive and sophisticated use of the mass communications media, and Congress' traditional reluctance to utilize the media, have tended to exalt the President and Administration as the prime movers in government in the public mind and, conversely, to diminish the role of Congress, thereby upsetting the Constitutional balance between the two branches.

3. Broader public access to the operations of Congress could stimulate Congressional awareness of the need to reform and modernize its rules and procedures and conduct the public business in a more efficient and effective manner.

4. Authority to broadcast floor proceedings would give to the electronic media, the principal source of news for the majority of Americans, a position equal to that of the print media which has enjoyed unrestricted access to floor proceedings.

5. Broadcasting of floor proceedings would, for the first time, assure a complete, accurate and unedited record of all that transpires on the House floor, both for historical purposes and contemporary use.

The Task Force also endorses the guidelines recommended by the Joint Committee for the pilot broadcast program. These guidelines would provide for: a rule-making supervisory authority to monitor and evaluate the test; an initial period of closed circuit broadcasts followed by video and audio feeds to commercial and public broadcasters for both live and delayed news programs; procedures to minimize interference with floor proceedings, to assure equitable and non-partisan coverage, and to facilitate expeditious actions on complaints; restrictions on the use of broadcast materials for political purposes and in commercial advertisements; and maintenance and availability of a complete and unedited collection of all the materials produced.

The Task Force believes the House is ready for this step toward open government. In 1970, the Legislative Reorganization Act encouraged broadcast coverage of Congressional committee hearings. In 1974, the House extended broadcast access to committee meetings. And just seven months ago, the House voted 358 to 25 to allow radio-TV coverage of the anticipated floor proceedings on impeachment.

Opening the chamber in which our laws are made to the eyes of all our citizens will help complete the process of bringing the Congress to the people.

SUSPENSION OF RULES

The Task Force recommends that the House rules be amended to more narrowly prescribe and limit the consideration of legislation under suspension of the rules.

This procedure was originally designed to permit the House to take up relatively noncontroversial bills reported from Committees by unanimous or near-unanimous vote. Debate time is limited to forty minutes, no amendments are permitted, and a two-thirds vote is required to suspend the rules and pass the bill. Prior to the 93rd Congress, the first and third Mondays of every month, and the last six days of a session were set aside for considering bills under this procedure.

At the beginning of the 93rd Congress, a new rule was reported from the Democratic Caucus to expand this to the first and third Tuesdays as well; and, near the close of the 93rd Congress, a resolution was offered by the Democratic leadership to permit consideration of bills under suspension from December ninth onward. In both of the above instances a majority of the Republican Members of the House voted against such expansions of the suspension procedure.

It is clear from the legislative record of the 93rd Congress that the more the suspension procedure is used, the more it is abused, to the detriment of sound legislative practice and results. The fact that numerous bills were defeated under suspension and that some were even cynically brought up under suspension for the very purpose of defeating them, is sufficient evidence that this procedure must be modified and restricted.

The Task Force, therefore, recommends that (a) suspension days again be reduced to two a month; (b) no bill be brought up under suspension unless the chairman and ranking minority member of a committee so request, or, unless two-thirds of the committee, by recorded vote, instructs the chairman to make such a request; (c) a dollar amount ceiling be placed on bills which may be brought up under suspension; (d) at least three calendar days advance notice (excluding Saturdays and Sundays) be given to any bill which is to be brought up under suspension; and (e) prior to scheduling a bill under suspension, the majority party leadership consult with minority leader.

While we do not favor the outright repeal of the suspension procedure and recognize its utility if limited to minor non-controversial legislation, we must strongly protest its increasing utilization for cynical purposes or on major, controversial bills. While our committees ordinarily do a thorough and responsible job on the legislation they report, their work should not be allowed to go unchallenged or unaltered on the House floor or to pass in substitute for the will of the House. The full and free working of the legislative process should not be sacrificed for the sake of expediency.

142

Congress meets to work its will upon legislation before it. It is the responsibility of the leadership to see that this is accomplished fairly, efficiently, and promptly and in accord with established principles of due process. A failure to do this because of inattention to duty or incompetence is an inexcusable reflection on the Congressional leadership. A failure to do so out of deliberate manipulation of the process is a reprehensible abuse of the public trust.

The legislation before the House of Representatives in the 93rd Congress was managed in a fashion embarrassing to every Member and to every knowledgeable American. For example:

Minor or routine business was often scheduled on Monday or Tuesday; Wednesday was then used for consideration of rules of scheduled debates; that left the House only Thursday to work on, and vote on, up to several major pieces of legislation. Debate was limited and deliberation abbreviated, because Members had to leave to meet previous commitments. Important questions were unanswered, and often unasked. Broad participation was thwarted. The legislation suffered.

Members were warned that a Friday schedule was probable, and business was actually scheduled only to be cancelled at the last minute, leaving Members without engagements in their districts and without official business in Washington.

Days, weeks and even months passed without floor consideration of any important legislation, and often without meetings of important committees. Then large numbers of major bills were scheduled immediately before a recess allowing too little time for proper consideration. In particular more bills than the House can reasonably handle were scheduled in June before the end of the fiscal year and in December before the end of the session.

Sessions of one or two hours were sometimes followed the next day by late night sessions. Every Member will work as late as is necessary to complete the business, but the marathon sessions are not conducive to careful consideration of legislation. Marathons do, and seemingly by design, limit debate.

Legislation was scheduled and then taken off the schedule at the last minute. The whole process was then repeated to the great inconvenience of the Members.

Legislation was brought up which had not even been placed on the schedule.

Legislation that could have been considered in a timely fashion was put off until late in the session. Frequently, legislation died because there was insufficient time to hold a conference or the bill was subject to a pre-adjournment filibuster in the Senate.

Committee work schedules had all the same problems, but magnified by the absolute power of chairmen. Routine, predictable business was ignored, delayed, held back, then processed wildly in marathon sessions called at the chairman's whim.

The Task Force recommends:

1. *The leadership should encourage prompt committee action* on all legislation by keeping well informed on the status of all legislation and by constantly urging early consideration.

2. *General work plans should be established* by committees in January for all substantive committees' regular or foreseeable work. These schedules should be published. Conflicts should be determined early and resolved promptly.

3. *A rule should be adopted prohibiting consideration of legislation not reported by a committee by a given (cut off) date.*

4. *Once a committee has reported legislation favorably, it becomes the responsibility of the leadership to provide for its prompt disposition. To this end we urge that the Rules of the House be amended to provide that:*

(a) All legislation which qualifies for the Suspension Calendar and is so reported must be placed at once upon the Suspension Calendar for action at the next succeeding suspension day, or referred to the Rules Committee.

(b) Legislation placed upon the Suspension Calendar shall be considered at the next suspension day or be withdrawn.

(c) Legislation defeated on suspension or withdrawn cannot thereafter be returned to the Suspension Calendar but must be immediately referred to either the originating committee or the Committee on Rules.

(d) Legislation referred to the Committee on Rules must be returned to the originating committee unless the Rules Committee takes favorable action thereon within thirty days.

(e) Resolutions of the Rules Committee requiring floor action shall be considered promptly. If such a Resolution and the bill to which it refers are not called up for floor action within thirty legislative days, the legislation under consideration must be returned automatically to the originating committee.

5. Reasonable notice of a legislative program is essential to its intelligent consideration and fundamental to due process of law. The Democratic leadership's failure to meet its obligation in this record is reflected all too frequently in the legislative product of the Congress.

We suggest the following changes as appropriate improvements in the scheduling of legislation before the House of Representatives in the 94th Congress:

(a) *Firm schedule published in the Congressional Record at least one week in advance of consideration.*

(b) *All bills to be considered by the full House placed on the schedule.*

(c) *Bills taken up in the approximate order they are granted a rule.*

(d) *Major legislation programmed for consideration at a time certain as to day and hours.*

(e) *Stringent compliance with the three-day rule concerning conference reports.*

(f) *No scheduling contingent on favorable recommendation of Rules Committee or any other committee.*

(g) *Publication of tentative commitments as to legislative schedule.*

(h) *Scheduling balanced so that Members can expect daily legislative sessions of reasonable uniform duration during any particular week.*

(i) *Delayed votes taken under the suspension calendar indicated on the schedule.*

6. The Task Force, in addition, urges the Congress to make a wide ranging study of scheduling procedures, including a detailed analysis of practices in other legislatures. The end product of this study shall be a comprehensive resolution on Congressional scheduling based on successful experiences in other deliberate bodies.

We endorse the early publication of the 1975 recess schedule and its generous allocation of home district time. But our praise carries with it two caveats: (1) The adjournment schedule, once set, must be adhered to; (2) The generous allocation of home district time requires full use of Fridays and Mondays for committee work, as well as for floor business.

While we applaud this small but significant step, we caution that it only assures orderliness in the district schedules of individual members. It is far more important to put orderliness into the handling of the people's business in the House Chamber and in our committees where chaos and disorder reign today.

CONGRESSIONAL RECORD REFORM

The Task Force believes the Congressional Record should reflect, accurately and authentically, what actually happens in the chambers of the House and Senate.

The Record does not do so because:

1. Remarks never spoken and material never seen by other Members at the time of debate are printed in the Record as though they were actually considered during that debate.

2. Words spoken in floor debate, sometimes having a significant bearing on the legislative history of a measure, can be eliminated from the printed record.

3. Complete statements and speeches of Members who were not even present for the debate are printed as part of the debate in a manner which makes it appear that they participated.

4. Other materials are inserted in the body of the Record, as

though the words were actually spoken on the floor, when, in fact, they were merely submitted for publication.

5. Hundreds of pages of the Record are filled with extraneous materials which bear no relationship to legislative issues.

6. Summaries of floor action are often incomplete or inaccurate, reports of committee meetings and hearings are sometimes uninformative, incomplete or missing entirely, while schedules of future committee meetings and hearings may similarly be incomplete or uninformative.

As a result, the legislative history of major legislation is often misleading as to Congressional intent. Both contemporary analysts of public policy and historians are denied an accurate record of the factors and arguments actually entering into Congressional decisions. The official record of Congressional activities becomes a less useful and reliable tool for Members, their staffs and the public alike.

To improve the accuracy and usefulness of the Record, the Task Force recommends that:

1. *Materials used to extend or supplement remarks actually delivered by Members be printed in a distinguishably different type.*

2. *Entire speeches or statements, no part of which were personally spoken during a debate or in special orders, be printed—again in a distinguishably different type face—at the conclusion of such debate.*

3. *Extraneous matter unrelated to legislative or public policy issues be eliminated from the Record.*

4. *The Daily Digest section of the Record be improved to assure completeness and accuracy of the information it contains.*

5. The House provide, and assure public access to, an accurate, unedited record of all that transpires on the House floor (see Broadcasting. (No. 7), recommendation No. 5).

CONGRESSIONAL NEWSLETTER FUNDS

Congressional newsletters perform the valuable function of educating and informing the general public about Congress and the political process. Newsletters, however, are not only a necessary and legitimate means of communicating with constituents, but they also serve as a powerful political device.

The source of funds for newsletter printing and distribution is both public and private. Newsletters may be mailed under the frank, but the costs of printing and addressing are required to be covered by other means. Some Members pay for newsletters out of their own pocket. Others use excess campaign funds. Still others set up "newsletter funds" financed by friendly organizations and individuals.

The status of these private sources of funds is ambiguous. Section 318 of the Federal Election Campaign Act of 1971, as amended, specifically authorizes candidates to use their excess campaign funds for newsletters, but requires that these expenditures be fully disclosed. Contributions to newsletter funds are eligible for tax credits and tax deductions. There does not appear to be, however, any other federal law regulating the sources or uses of such funds. Candidates may accept unlimited contributions from any individual or organization (including labor unions or corporations) without disclosing the amount or source of such funds.

The present situation is clearly unacceptable. The Task Force recommends that Congress immediately:

1. *Require full disclosure of the sources of all contributions to and the nature of all expenditures from funds for newsletters and other so-called institutional outlays between campaigns.*

2. *Prohibit labor unions and corporations from giving to these funds.*

3. *Limit contributions to these funds to $1,000 per person.*

The American people have shown their desire for full public disclosure of all sources of funds used to pay for both political and official business. The Congress should extend disclosure requirements to include newsletter and other such similar funds.

BINDING CAUCUS INSTRUCTIONS: "THE UNIT RULE"

The Task Force unequivocally opposes the imposition of binding caucus instructions and proposes that this practice be prohibited by the Rules of the House of Representatives.

While this "unit rule" is unique to the Democratic Caucus, as Members of the other party, we would ordinarily not presume to interfere with the internal operation of the Democratic Party Caucus. In this instance, we have, however, a clear obligation to object as this practice directly affects the rights of the House and the integrity of its proceedings.

By means of the "unit rule", as few as one-third of the Members of the Democratic Caucus can dictate procedural and substantive matters in the various committees and may well determine the legislative outcome on the House Floor. This is a most serious if not unconstitutional, affront to our democratic system. Allegiance to the Caucus, under the "unit rule" procedure, takes precedence over one's conscience and the needs of one's constituencies.

Moreover, this practice completely nullifies the gains we have made in making the legislative system more accountable for it places the real decision-making powers in secret caucus sessions utilizing secret ballot voting.

We are not fooled by attempts to differentiate between questions of procedure and substance. Procedural votes on the previous question or a closed rule shape a bill as much as any substantive amendment. Indeed Rules of the House are adopted on a procedural vote and they determine, in many cases, whether important bills will pass or fail.

Finally, caucus imposition of binding instructions is an insult to the intelligence of every Member of the House and to the collective expertise inherent in our committee system. It is a worse insult to the electorate. In short, it is a poor substitute for real leadership, for full, free and open deliberations, and for independent and prudent decision-making.

MINORITY STAFFING

The Task Force wholeheartedly endorses proposals to provide the minority party members with up to one-third of total committee staff. During the last Congress, the Minority had less than 10% of the staff of many committees, and averages less than 15% of the staff of all committees.

Adequate committee staffing, for both the majority and minority parties, is essential to the effectiveness of the legislative process. Insufficient staffing for the minority party ultimately worked to the disadvantage of both parties. Many Democrats joined Republicans in recognizing the validity of this principle when the House, on July 16, 1970, voted 105–63 to allow one-third of committee investigatory funds to be used for staff for the Minority. However, before the 1970 Legislative Reorganization Act embodying this change went into effect, the Democratic majority—including many who had previously voted for minority staffing—stripped away the provisions for broadened minority staffing.

Last year, the House clearly reaffirmed its original position by amending H. Res. 988 to provide the Minority of each committee with one-third of both the investigative and professional staff funds. Once again, the Democratic majority reversed the will of the full House and exhibited its skill at staff stealing by eliminating the provision allotting the minority of up to one-third of each committee's investigative staff. While the Task Force is gratified by the Democratic majority's generosity in granting the Minority a sizable increase in committee staff, it is disappointed that once again, the Minority has been deprived of its full entitlement to committee staff positions.

A wide spectrum of observers of the legislative process—Common Cause, Ralph Nader, prominent, academic, and noted professional experts, among others—favor adequate minority staffing. Ample reasons have been given to support this position:

1. Without adequate minority representation, committee staffs tend to reflect only one side of the issue—usually the views of the employing Member. Resulting legislation mirrors this basis and consequently can have serious shortcomings. As an example, many of the Great Society programs pushed through Congress in the mid-1960's might have been more successful if their enthusiastic initiation had

been accompanied by more well-articulated input by the programs, lacked sufficient staff to demonstrate these defects convincingly. Certain of these programs wasted millions of the taxpayers' dollars; and public support for them subsequently diminished. In the end, the Majority was held politically responsible for these failures.

2. Sufficient minority staffing will help revive the adversary process. This process, of course, depends upon the best possible presentation of all facets of an issue. Both the minority and the majority need adequate staff resources to grapple with the complex issues of contemporary society. Without adequate minority staffing, the majority remains unencumbered by disturbing but valid opposing points of view. In the final analysis, both the legislative process and the Nation are the losers.

3. Minority staffing need not encourage partisan rancor. With enough staff to explore, develop and express different solutions to legislative problems, Majority and Minority will be better able to understand each other's viewpoints and work together toward constructive, well-considered results.

4. Increased minority staffing should aid Congress in becoming a more effective branch of Government. A minority deprived of staffing is tempted to rely on outside resources—the Executive Branch or private groups and interests.

In conclusion, adequate minority staffing fosters the development of the adversary process of legislation, increases policy alternatives, provides stimulus for generating excellent legislation, and strengthens Congress as a branch of Government. The result is a quality of legislation of which both Democrats and Republicans can be proud.

Single party, monolithic, winner-take-all control of legislative resources may be tolerated in elitist societies, but it should not be in ours. The Task Force urges that the minority be entitled to a full one-third of all committee staff positions.

TOTAL ELIMINATION OF PROXY VOTING

On October 8, 1974, the House voted 196–166 for an amendment to completely ban proxy voting in House committees. That amendment was incorporated into "The Committee Reform Amendments of 1974" which overwhelmingly passed by a vote of 359–7 that same day. In the secrecy of their caucus only three months later, House Democrats reversed that decision. House Republicans have solidly endorsed the elimination of proxy voting without qualification both in committee and on the floor and have vigorously opposed House Democrats' efforts to restore this anti-reform at the beginning of this Congress.

In Committee, Republicans have introduced motions to prohibit proxy voting. In virtually every case, the vote has split along party lines. Democrats have solidly supported government by absentee ballot." In the fourteen committees organized so far in this Congress, the Democrats have voted 392 times for proxies.

The Task Force finds proxy voting a process unworthy of a representatives body, destructive of public confidence, and counter-productive to our goal of producing the best possible legislation. Specifically, we find that:

1. Members of Congress are elected by their constituents to represent them in all respects of the legislative process. The transfer of that obligation to another person is abhorrent to, and inconsistent with, our representative form of government. Just as corporation directors and trustees are prohibited by common law from giving their representatives votes by proxy, elected Representatives should also be prohibited from voting by proxy.

2. Active participation in committee work—the acquisition of information, discussion, debate and mark up of a bill is as important as voting. The proxy system allows less active members to give the appearance of voting without fulfilling their obligation to prepare and participate personally.

3. Proxies reinforce the potential for abuse already inherent in the current unwholesome system which relies on the excessive powers of Committee chairmen. The Task Force believes that the majority party has grossly overendowed committee chairmen with life-and-death power over legislation. Proxies can make it possible for legislation to reflect a chairman's whim rather than solid legislative consideration.

4. Proxies sustain a system which allows certain privileged, senior Members to serve on more than one major committee, despite the conflicting time demands and workloads of those committees. This proxy-supported scheme gives favored Members an unfair measure of control over a broad range of legislation, and proportionately dilutes the strength of other Members not enjoying these privileges.

5. Proxies, because they are increasingly subject to abuse, contribute to public cynicism and reduce confidence in the legislative process.

6. Proxies encourage sloppy scheduling. Unbusinesslike scheduling in the House is a disgrace. Use of proxies takes away the principal incentive for orderly and timely scheduling of House business.

Even though the rules of the 93rd Congress encouraged proxy voting, some committees (Appropriations, Rules and Banking and Currency) abolished this practice without any noticeable negative effects on the legislative process. The successful effort of the Democratic majority to reinstate proxy voting is a prime example of backtracking on reform.

APPORTIONMENT OF COMMITTEES

The House Democratic Caucus has demanded that Democrats be represented on all committees of the House by a ratio of 2–1, plus one. Republicans originally did not object, because of the unfounded belief that the ratio would apply only to full committees. Unfortunately, this ratio has been applied to all subcommittees and conference committees as well.

In binding all Democrats under a "unit rule", the Caucus easily implemented this unfair ratio while the Speaker was similarly bound. Rules brought to the floor, under such despotic procedure, prohibited Republicans from offering amendments.

The discriminatory nature of the two-thirds plus-one rule has been dramatically exposed in subcommittee assignment and in potential conference committee assignments. Subcommittees, under this rule, must be 7–3 or 9–4, and the unfairness of the plus one magnifies the majority percentage from 67 to 70%. On conference committees, especially the critical tax conferences, where House delegates are traditionally small, the proportions are worse. Suggestions have already been made for 3–1 or 5–2 ratios which would destroy equity by raising Democrat ratios as high as 75%.

Republican participation on conference committees, under the ⅔ plus 1 requirement, would invariably be limited to one, at best, two Members. This unduly limits the spectrum of Republican viewpoints which can be represented. Minority Members advocating a blend of differing positions on an issue would be excluded from conference committee participation by the imposition of this unfair ratio. This severely limits the presentation of minority views and increases the likelihood of unchallenged, steamrollered laws.

We, therefore, urge that the rule be discarded in favor of one requiring ratios which generally conform to the ratios in the House itself and that the Speaker and Minority Leader be empowered to exchange committee positions depending on current requests of their caucuses.

QUORUMS

The Task Force firmly opposes any effort to reduce the number of Members needed to constitute a quorum in committee meetings. Any new rule subverting the standard quorum in House committees will only debase the democratic process, reduce the incentives for broad-based participation and cast public doubt on the legislative product of this body. The proposal for reducing the number of Members needed to constitute a quorum endorses increased absenteeism and non-participation. It is necessitated by the present system allowing certain favored Democratic Members to have multiple assignments on key committees.

The Task Force urges the Democratic caucus to make proposals which will serve to democratize House proceedings, instead of those which only narrow the base of participation. Now is not the time to produce rule changes which will increase the dominance of House committee and subcommittee chairmen while serving as an inducement for Members to stay home and rest.

ORDER FORMS

Please tear out and mail your order to:
EPM Publications, Inc., Box 442, McLean, Va. 22101 (phone 703-356-5111)

Please send me _____ paperback books of "THE FUTILE SYS-TEM" by John J. Rhodes.
1 copy $2.35, 10 copies $18 00, 100 copies $160.00
(Price includes postage and handling)
Virginia residents only, add 4% sales tax.
Please enclose your check or money order.

Name_____
   (Please Print)   First   Initial   Last

Street_____
               P. O. Box, or Apt. Number

City   State   Zip

Please tear out and mail your order to:
EPM Publications, Inc., Box 442, McLean, Va. 22101 (phone 703-356-5111)

Please send me _____ paperback books of "THE FUTILE SYS-TEM" by John J. Rhodes.
1 copy $2.35, 10 copies $18 00, 100 copies $160.00
(Price includes postage and handling)
Virginia residents only, add 4% sales tax.
Please enclose your check or money order.

Name_____
   (Please Print)   First   Initial   Last

Street_____
               P. O. Box, or Apt. Number

City   State   Zip

EPM Publications, Inc., Box 442, McLean, Va. 22101

EPM Publications, Inc., Box 442, McLean, Va. 22101

"One glance tells you," a leading columnist has written, "God had a Congressman in mind when He made John Rhodes."

A native Kansan, Rhodes located in Arizona following his service in World War II. He graduated from Harvard Law School and in 1952 became the first Republican elected to the House from Arizona. He has served there longer than anyone in Arizona history.

After being chairman of the House Republican Policy Committee, Rhodes moved up to the top GOP leadership post in 1973 when Gerald R. Ford became Vice President. In a party marked by fierce leadership struggles he was first in 40 years to be elected unanimously. He guided his party through the treacherous shoals of the impeachment inquiry and was unanimously reelected as Minority Leader at the start of the 94th Congress.

Not content to rest on past accomplishments, Rhodes now wants to become Speaker. He knows that his party will have to fight back from near-death in order to win control of the House. In THE FUTILE SYSTEM he sets forth the blueprint for that victory— as well as for the vital reforms that only such a victory can ensure.

Photograph by George Tames, *The New York Times*